CRIME IN INDIA

CRIME IN INDIA

A Brief Review of the more Important Offences included in the A inual Criminal Returns with Chapters on Prostitution & Miscellaneous Malters

by

S. M. EDWARDES, C.S.I., C.V.O.

GYAN

Published by

GYAN

Gyan Publishing House
5, Ansari Road
Daryaganj, New Delhi-110002
Phone: 011-47034999, 9811692060
E-mail: books@gyanbooks.com

Distribution Network
gyanbooks.com
India, USA, Canada, UK, Australia, France

ISBN : 978-81-212-6016-9 (PB)
First Published, 1924

2nd Impression 2021

Printed at: Gyan Press, Delhi.

Crime in India
Author: S. M. Edwardes

CRIME
IN INDIA

A Brief Review of the more Important Offences included in the Annual Criminal Returns with Chapters on Prostitution & Miscellaneous Matters

BY

S. M. EDWARDES, C.S.I., C.V.O.

HUMPHREY MILFORD
OXFORD UNIVERSITY PRESS
LONDON NEW YORK TORONTO MELBOURNE
CAPE TOWN BOMBAY CALCUTTA MADRAS
1924

PREFACE

THIS book cannot lay claim to be in any so if an exhaustive survey of the crime committed year by year in India. Such a work would fill three or more volumes of tolerable size, and would in parts be extraordinarily dull. For the ordinary crime of a minor character, which appears in the annual police reports and schedules, is very uninspiring, and, if we allow for differences of race, religion and climate, differs little from offences of the same type in other countries. I have, therefore, confined my remarks to the major offences common in India, endeavouring to illustrate their nature, frequency and special characteristics by concrete cases, chosen from the annual official reports of crime during recent years. Inasmuch as the book deals solely with modern crime, all reference to the notorious criminal organizations of a vanished age, such as the Thags, has been omitted, and for the sake of simplicity the headings and contents of the first three chapters have been based on the classification followed in modern Indian statistics and reports.

The fourth chapter deals briefly with the history and present features of Prostitution in India, which, though it cannot be properly described as a criminal offence, is nevertheless closely connected with crime and police work. Moreover, I am not aware that this subject, which of late years has attracted the increased attention of Indian reformers and European administrators, has been discussed and explained in any single and easily accessible work. The article of Dr. W. Crooke, in Hastings' *Encyclopædia of Religion and*

Ethics, gives a succinct and valuable *résumé* of Indian prostitution in past centuries, upon which I have drawn freely in my remarks on the historical aspect of the question; while the facts in regard to modern prostitution are based upon the knowledge acquired as the head of an important urban police force.

In the fifth chapter I have included a variety of miscellaneous matters which are more or less directly connected with crime in India. I consider it unnecessary to deal separately with political crime, as those who wish to understand the lengths to which the Indian anarchist or agitator will go, if unchecked, can consult such authoritative records as the Report of the Rowlatt Committee on Sedition, published in 1918, and other official publications. I have, however, drawn pointed attention, wherever necessary, to the effect upon crime of the deplorable political agitation of the last few years, and have also laid stress in the final chapter on the gulf which lies between the aspirations of the Indian *intelligentsia* and the mental and moral outlook of the general body of the population. I shall consider myself amply compensated for the labour of compiling this modest volume, if it serves to enlighten the ignorant on the important and wholly admirable part played by the Indian police, under their European superintendents and Indian officers, during the grave disorders of the last few years.

London, 1924. S. M. EDWARDES

CONTENTS

CHAPTER I

OFFENCES AGAINST THE STATE

COUNTERFEIT COINING

THE manufacture of counterfeit rupees and coins of smaller value is a constant offence in India, and is often carried out by tribes or gangs of professional false coiners, such as the Baurias, who wander all over India, and the Chhaparbands, who were notorious in the Bombay Presidency until the Government commenced an attempt to reclaim them from their criminal habits. The style and finish of the counterfeit coin varies considerably. At times false rupees have appeared in circulation, which almost required the eye of an expert for their detection; on the other hand, some of the coins made in rough moulds by the nomadic criminal tribes are so poor that only the ignorance and gullibility of the ordinary villager renders their circulation possible. The police wage perpetual war against false coiners and forgers of currency notes, and are frequently successful in seizing collections of false coins, moulds and apparatus. In the United Provinces in 1921, 59 cases were placed before the courts; in Rangoon in the same year the police discovered 1,500 counterfeit rupees, 50 moulds and 3 sets of apparatus; in the Panjab there were 20 cases, in one of which a gang of Bauria coiners was betrayed by a jealous woman of the tribe, who boasted that her clan were counterfeiting coin all over India in the disguise of *fakirs* and *sadhus* (*scil.* Musalman and Hindu professional mendicants). The Bombay

City Police prosecuted thirteen cases in 1921, and in the previous year the Behar and Orissa police arrested a gang which was manufacturing eight-anna, four-anna and two-anna pieces. In the Bombay Presidency counterfeit coining, as well as the forgery of currency notes, is constantly occurring, and the notes are occasionally so well made as to deceive the average man in the street. The North-West Frontier Police unearthed a considerable manufacture of five-rupee notes in 1921, while in the Central Provinces during the same year 56 cases of counterfeiting were successfully brought to trial, and three gangs of Baurias were sentenced to varying terms of imprisonment.

A remarkable case of false coining occurred in Nagpur. The official staff of the Central Jail suddenly became aware that one of their prisoners was gaily counterfeiting four-anna and two-anna pieces *inside the jail.* He was promptly prosecuted and was sentenced to a term of rigorous imprisonment; but on appeal the Sessions Judge quashed the conviction, as he found it impossible to believe that the prisoner could have counterfeited coin in the presence of so many prisoners and under the nose of the jail staff. Against the acquittal of the prisoner by the Sessions Judge the Local Government made a further appeal, which resulted in the original finding and sentence being restored. One can hardly imagine the possibility of a long-term convict in, say, Maidstone Jail calmly counterfeiting sixpenny and threepenny bits, and it seems possible that jail supervision and discipline in India are sometimes of a more *dolce far niente* type than is usual in England. If the average Indian peasant and small trader were less gullible and more alert, a good deal of false coining and note-forgery would automatically cease.

The extent to which deception can be practised upon them is shown by the fact that at the height of the subversive *Khilafat* agitation many *Khilafat* 'notes' were palmed off with genuine currency notes upon unsuspicious and illiterate people, who did not discover their mistake until they attempted to change them in the bazaars. Shortly before the outbreak of the War (1914-18) a retail dealer in Bombay imported from Japan a consignment of very fine white silk handkerchiefs, bearing in the centre a beautifully executed facsimile of the Indian ten-rupee currency note. The reproduction was so perfect that a clever cheat, by treatment and manipulation of the handkerchiefs, might conceivably have imposed upon the unsuspecting and ignorant. To avoid any *contretemps* of this kind, it was decided to confiscate the consignment and forbid the sale of similar goods.

Forgery

Forgery and the manufacture of false documents are also not infrequent offences in India, and courts before which civil suits regarding land or hereditary rights are filed have frequently to consider very carefully the authenticity of documents produced in support of the parties' claims. Cheque forgeries are not rare. In 1920 the Military Accounts Department, Bombay, discovered the forgery of a cheque for Rs. 23,000; in the same year four Bengalis in Calcutta conspired to cheat a local bank by means of a forged cheque for Rs. 50,000. The culprits in both cases were duly arrested. In 1921 the police of the North-West Frontier Province became aware that large numbers of forged railway tickets were being sold to passengers at much less than the sanctioned rate. Inquiry showed that the forgeries were perpetrated by an individual residing in Independent Territory across the border, and after some delay the police contrived to secure the type letters and figures used in the preparation of the false tickets. A Hindu, who commenced by personating a plaintiff in the Small Causes Court, Bombay, forged a document of the court for the purpose of obtaining a warrant for execution, and a European ne'er-do-weel contrived to obtain two sums of Rs. 1,800 and Rs. 1,500 from an Indian bank, by giving as security documents which had been cleverly fabricated. A few years ago a blank cheque was stolen from the premises of a well-known English mercantile firm by one of its Hindu employees, who then filled in the cheque for Rs. 10,900 and forged the signature of one of the principals of the firm. This done, he set fire to the firm's premises, which were almost destroyed, and having thus obliterated, as he believed, all trace of his crime, he cashed the cheque at a local bank. The police, however, discovered sufficient evidence against him to justify his being placed before a magistrate, who duly committed him for trial at the Sessions, where a peculiarly stupid jury, failing to appreciate the evidence and despite the Judge's remarks, gave a verdict of 'not guilty.'

A curious case occurred in Bombay in 1916. The military authorities at Basra complained that several followers of the Supply and Transport Corps, who had despatched various sums from Bombay to their relatives by money-order, found, after leaving Bombay, that they had been defrauded. Their suspicions were first aroused by noticing that, while their money-order receipts were in order on the obverse, the carbon impression on the reverse showed that the full amounts had not been sent. The money-order receipts, which were forwarded to the police with the formal complaint, revealed the fact that, while the full sum to be remitted and the correct commission thereon had been entered on the obverse, the carbon entry on the back of each receipt was for a smaller sum and a correspondingly smaller commission. Closer examination showed that the receipts had been tampered with. Several of the defrauded followers were summoned from Basra, and after investigation the police arrested at Lucknow an Anglo-Indian (*scil.* Eurasian), who had travelled to Bombay in charge of the followers. He was proved to have offered to despatch the money for the men to their relatives up-country; and having prepared a list of the amounts which each wished to send, he collected the total sum from the men, together with the amount due for the money-order commission. Proceeding to the General Post Office, he filled in the necessary money-order forms, substituting in each a smaller sum than that collected. These smaller sums were despatched and receipts obtained for them; but before handing these receipts over to the men, the accused altered the figures to correspond with the original sums which he had been entrusted to despatch. Had he taken the precaution of placing a piece of blue carbon paper below each receipt as he changed the figures, the probabilities are that the fraud would not have been noticed. The accused was sentenced to a term of imprisonment.

Considerable ingenuity characterised a fraud reported by the Central Telegraph Office, Bombay, in 1921. The departmental authorities suddenly discovered that messages despatched from a certain sub-office in the city had been paid for by previously-used stamps, which had been cleverly cut up and pieced together. The money accepted for these messages had been misappropriated. It appeared on enquiry that eighty-four messages received from the Check Office in Calcutta had thus been paid for by reconstructed stamps. The police compiled a statement of dates, times, and the names of clerks who disposed of these messages, and were thus able to fix responsibility upon two men, who were duly convicted, and also upon a stamp-dealer at Karachi, who was found in possession of a tin trunk filled with used stamps in various stages of reconstruction.

Personating a Public Servant

A certain number of cases occur annually, in which offences are perpetrated by persons unlawfully assuming the guise and functions of public servants. More often than not the criminal personates a police officer, in the belief that his chance of attaining his end is thereby increased. This belief must have weighed with two European loafers who, posing as detectives, attempted to blackmail an Indian by threats of charging him with an attempt to commit an unnatural offence with a European boy. The time and place of their attempted extortion were well chosen; but the Indian fortunately had sufficient courage to withstand their demands and make an open complaint to the police, who had no difficulty in arresting both the men and the boy, and securing their conviction at the Sessions. A bad character, who was charged with personation in the Central Provinces in 1921, showed himself to be possessed of a sense of humour. He suddenly disappeared from surveillance, after stealing the instruments and outfit of a public vaccinator.

Armed with these, he made his way to a neighbouring district, where he proceeded solemnly to vaccinate, or pretend to vaccinate, all the children in the neighbourhood, supporting himself comfortably during the operation on the free doles of food and other necessaries supplied by the villagers. He was fortunately arrested after seven days' hard work with the lancet.

FALSE COMPLAINTS; FALSE EVIDENCE; FALSE SUITS

False complaints and false cases are a well-established feature of Indian life, as the annual police and magisterial returns amply testify; and while many of such cases may be due to mistake of fact, an uncomfortably large number are properly classed as 'maliciously false.' The false complaint supported by false evidence is one of the means most commonly employed to wreak revenge on an enemy, and the false story is sometimes concocted with such devilish ingenuity that it is difficult for magistrate or police officer to decide where the truth lies. It is this wide-spread habit of launching false prosecutions and suborning false witnesses that underlies the objection of European residents in India to being tried by Indian criminal courts without being granted special safeguards, and it is certain that some of those Europeans who live almost alone in remote country-tracts, in charge of factories or tea-gardens, would, especially in times of political unrest, be exposed to grave harassment and annoyance, if they were not protected by special provisions of the laws of criminal procedure. It is not so very long ago that the European owner of a large landed estate in India, with whom certain villagers were at loggerheads, found himself falsely charged with inciting to an unlawful assembly, and was forced to spend a large sum of money in barrister's fees and in appeals to a higher jurisdiction, before the false accusation could be disproved. False complaints against Europeans, however, are fortunately not very numerous and are greatly outnumbered by those laid by Indians against their own countrymen. In Bengal, for example, 1,752 maliciously false cases were recorded in 1917; 421 in Assam in 1921; 1,830 in Behar and Orissa in 1920; and 1,587 in the Bombay Presidency in the same year. The prosecution of those who lay false complaints is not always possible, and even where the prosecution ends in conviction, Indian magistrates are often very backward in awarding compensation to those who have been falsely accused.

As might well be supposed from the general attitude of the Indian public towards the police, the latter are specially liable to be falsely accused of acts of tyranny and extortion, and it is probably only the knowledge that any such complaint will be closely investigated by the constable's superior officers, and may be followed by legal reprisals, which prevents the wholesale fabrication of charges against the force. As evidence of the extent to which Indians will attempt to use the law thus falsely, the case of a police sub-inspector at Kishenganj, in Behar and Orissa, may be quoted. He was deliberately accused of culpable homicide, attempt to extort a confession, wrongful confinement and corruption. These various charges were closely investigated, and were clearly proved, one and all, to be deliberately false. A case happened in Bengal, in which the police who were conducting an investigation were suddenly attacked by a mob of villagers, who subsequently laid a false charge of dacoity against them and supported it with wholesale false evidence. Thirty-three false charges were laid against the police of Assam in 1921, which ranged from accusations of torture and bribery to such minor offences as hurt, assault and wrongful confinement.

Though the law provides for the punishment of those who accuse others falsely, its provisions are frequently defeated by the great delay which takes place in obtaining the sanction of higher authority for the prosecution of the offender and in the subsequent hearing of the case. Thus, in a case reported false by the police on May 10 in a certain year, sanction to proceed against the offender was not received till the middle of the following July, and the case was still pending before the court in December. In another case reported as false in July, sanction to prosecute had not been received by the close of the year. Such delays almost invariably prevent the prosecution being brought to a successful issue, and, where the courts are concerned, are usually due to the granting of remands on flimsy or inadequate grounds, to the latitude allowed in cross-examination, and to the portentous length of the addresses delivered by counsel and *vakils* (pleaders).

False civil suits, which have earned an unenviable notoriety in the City of Bombay, are similarly the product of a desire to cause loss and annoyance to an enemy. It is a common practice, especially in the United Provinces, for designing persons to file suits at some distant place against those to whom they bear a grudge. The defendant has to choose between two evils. Either he must go and contest the suit, which means a great waste of money and time, or he must accept the alternative of an *ex-parte* decree against himself. A considerable number of such false suits have of late years been filed in Bombay, and the investigation which the police have to make, in order to prove their falsity, is usually tedious and complex. Lengthy correspondence has to be carried on with the police of another province, and when the suit is heard, the witnesses have to be summoned from their distant homes to Bombay. The suit having been rejected, an application has to be made to the court for sanction to prosecute, and this is followed by the prosecution of the plaintiff. These proceedings, even in the most favourable circumstances, last for months, and make very heavy inroads upon the defendant's time and pocket.

The following is a typical instance of this class of offence. A Marwadi *shroff* of Bombay, named Narsi Tekchand, one day filed a suit in the Small Causes Court for the recovery of Rs. 701 from two persons, Sahebdin Ramdat Pathak, resident in the Jaunpur District of the United Provinces, and Rawal Nana Shankar. When process was served on the first defendant, Sahebdin, in his village, he reported to the police of the district that the suit was false, and the matter was at once reported to the Bombay Police for further inquiry. In the course of their investigation the Bombay Criminal Investigation Department discovered that the name of the second defendant was fictitious, and that Narsi Tekchand had been persuaded to file the suit by one Jaikishora Sharma, who bore enmity towards Sahebdin Ramdat. Sanction to prosecute both Narsi Tekchand and his accomplice, Jaikishora, was obtained, and Sahebdin Ramdat eventually had the satisfaction of seeing Narsi Tekchand convicted and sentenced to four months' rigorous imprisonment and a fine of Rs. 200, and Jaikishora Sharma sentenced to six months' rigorous imprisonment. The false civil suit is well-known in Bengal, where, on the occasion of a dispute between a landholder and his tenant regarding the possession of a village, no less than thirty-one false suits were instituted by the relatives of the landholder against the tenant and his supporters. In such ways are our elaborate civil courts and procedure utilized to secure the embarrassment of an enemy.

RIOTING

Rioting and unlawful assembly have been of frequent occurrence in India during the last century and more. But until the last few years most of the riots were due to agrarian disputes or to the fundamental sectarian hostility existing between Hindus and Muhammadans. These causes still operate, for most of the 588 outbreaks in Bengal in 1917, and of the 470 outbreaks in Behar and Orissa in 1920, were directly caused by disputes about land, while year by year the authorities consider themselves fortunate if great Moslem festivals, like the *Muharram* and *Bakri Id*, pass off without a fanatical outbreak of disturbance. Up to the year 1911, when the Commissioner of Police contrived by a two-fold policy of force and persuasion to put an end permanently to the great *Muharram* processions through the city, the celebration of that festival in Bombay had earned an unenviable reputation for lawlessness and disorder. The predisposing cause was the hostility of the Sunni sects to the Shiah Bohras, coupled with the intolerable license displayed by the *tolis* or bands, varying in numbers from 30 to 500, which accompanied the *tabuts* and *tazias* in their perambulation of the streets. The festival had also degenerated into an occasion of blackmail on a large scale, levied by the lowest classes of Muhammadans upon Hindus, chiefly of the trading and shop-keeping class. Any fancied grievance during the first few days of the festival was eagerly exploited by the wire-pullers in the Muhammadan quarters, and served as an excuse for an outbreak of violence on the tenth day, which had frequently to be drastically quelled by the police and troops of the garrison. It is only in the City of Bombay, however, that the processional portion of the *Muharram* festival has ceased to take place. Elsewhere the mimic tombs of Husein and Hassan are carried through the streets and lanes of the towns, as they have been since Mughal days, and the local police have their hands full with the task of keeping order along the route and preventing an outbreak of disorder. The *Bakri Id*, which commemorates according to Moslem views the sacrifice of Ishmael by Abraham, is well calculated to arouse the hostility of the Hindu population; for cattle, sheep and goats are slaughtered wholesale by the Muhammadans; and in many parts of India this commemorative sacrifice of cattle leads to violent hostilities between Moslem and Hindu.

People in England have no conception of the overwhelming religious antagonism which this festival can arouse, and are not much assisted to a better understanding of the matter by the London Press. One of the leading newspapers in 1923 informed its readers that the *Bakri Id* was a festival in honour of 'Bakri, a writer of devotional verse.' A few weeks later an illustrated daily paper referred to the *Muharram* as 'the Muhrami, a festival in honour of Hobson-Jobson, the grandson of the Prophet'! It occasionally happens that Moslem festivals, which are constantly shifting in accordance with the Muhammadan lunar calendar, coincide with important Hindu festivals, like the *Holi*, which is particularly notorious for ribaldry and licence. On such occasions the probability of disturbance is increased, and the experienced police official is compelled to keep in reserve a considerable force of armed men. If a *Muharram* mob once gets out of hand and commences looting and assaulting pedestrians and stopping all traffic, it is the wisest, and in the end the kindest, course to fire upon it at once, after giving reasonable warning. The firing of blank cartridge is a fatal mistake, for it merely exasperates the mob and incites it to further excesses. Some of the serious disturbances of recent years would have been more rapidly quelled, and with far less loss of life than actually occurred, had the police only felt they would be fully supported by the Government in resorting without delay to rifle-fire.

While disputes about land and religious fanaticism will continue without doubt to form the *motif* of occasional outbursts of lawlessness, it is to be hoped that some limit has been placed upon the appalling exhibitions of disorder arising out of sheer political propaganda, which have sullied the name of India during the last ten or fifteen years. This series of disturbances, which are at bottom revolutionary and designed to embarrass and weaken the Government, though they occassionally assume an economic aspect, may be held to have commenced with the somewhat abortive Tilak riots of 1908 in Bombay. On that occasion a large proportion of the industrial population of the city, in consequence of mendacious propaganda disseminated among them by agents of Bal G. Tilak and his party, left their work and spent a tumultuous week in destroying mill-property and attacking police and troops. After that year there was a lull until 1917, when Home Rule Leaguers, Musalman *Khilafat* agitators and M. K. Ghandi's non-co-operators gradually combined to bring about a deplorable outburst of lawlessness, which manifested itself in continual rioting, jail outbreaks, industrial disturbances of a grave character, in the terrible Mappilla rebellion in Malabar, and in the still active Akali Sikh movement in the Panjab. In 1921 the Panjab recorded 860 cases of rioting; the United Provinces, 1,290 cases; the Central Provinces, 398 cases; all of them directly caused by political agitation and seditious propaganda. The large cities have suffered equally with the rural tracts. Lawlessness attained such a pitch in Calcutta during the Viceroyalty of Lord Chelmsford that the citizens, European and Indian, had to band themselves together to keep the peace and prevent constant picketing and *hartals* (stoppage of business); Madras was in the throes of disturbance for weeks; while Bombay's contribution to the general disorder culminated in the disgraceful rioting on the occasion of the Prince of Wales' arrival in India, when a mob of the lowest type practically controlled the central portion of the city for two days, and minorities like the Parsis and Native Christians, finding that they could not count at once upon adequate protection by the authorities, were forced to seize arms wherever they could and defend themselves and their women against the rabble.

The fundamental difference between what may be styled normal Indian rioting, connected with agrarian disputes or ancient religious animosity, and the political rioting to which India has become painfully accustomed during the last few years, lies in the attitude of the mob towards the police. In ordinary rioting of the first type the police intervene merely as guardians of law and order between two or more conflicting parties, and, though in the process of restoring peace they may be attacked, as usually happened in Bombay at *Muharram* riots, yet there was no general mass attack upon them, nor on the whole was any greater hostility shown to them than was necessarily engendered by their obvious determination to prevent the spread of disorder. But in the grave disturbances, engineered by political agitators during recent times, the primary object of the mob has been to attack and kill the police at all costs. Nothing has been more deplorable than the savage hatred displayed in the tragedies of the last few years towards men whose only fault was their fidelity to duty; and no praise is too high for the unflinching resolution and courage with which the police, whether at Aligarh, Bareilly, Chauri-Chaura, Bombay, Sholapur, Madras, Kumbakonam, or other centres, faced most desperate situations. That fact alone should have reminded the Indian Government that a stern policy of repression of lawlessness was one of the surest methods of rewarding these humble servants, as well as of vindicating their own position.

The ordeal through which the police of India passed with entire credit to themselves during the period of five or six years prior to March, 1922, is well illustrated by the following excerpt from the Police Report of the Madras Presidency for the year 1921:

> 'They were opposed with violence, threatened, widely abused from platforms, called traitors to their country and the myrmidons of her tyrants, insulted in public, made the butt of ribald songs, sometimes spat upon, sometimes boycotted,

sometimes cajoled and appealed to, to desert their service; and perhaps, most of all, they felt, in the days when Government out of tolerance to the non-co-operation movement made no firm stand, that their position was not sure, that Government's steadfastness was uncertain. In spite of all this, they stood firm and showed a fine restraint and forbearance.'

In some districts, where constant assaults were made on the police in 1921, their position was further undermined by the attitude of the Indian magistracy. In Hissar, for example, at the moment when police stations were being attacked by mobs and the public respect for authority was rapidly declining, the magistrates were inclined to adopt an incredulous or unduly lenient attitude in many of the cases of assaults on the police which were placed before them. Some of these assaults took place when the police were engaged in their regular duties, notably when effecting the arrest of persons charged with enticing away a married woman for improper purposes. In Assam the unjustifiable acquittal by a magistrate of a gang of persons who had committed a political dacoity led to unfortunate results. Two attempts were made upon the life of the police-officer who investigated the case, and a series of dacoities in Sylhet and Mymensingh were subsequently perpetrated by the same gang. The police of this province were further handicapped by their inadequate armament—the bored-out Martini musket, which is obsolete and useless for dealing efficiently with mobs bent upon murder, arson and the indiscriminate destruction of property. In cases where the police were forced to fire in self-defence, they were lucky if they escaped being charged with murder. This happened to a sub-inspector of the Bengal Police, who was in charge of a party carrying out the search of a house, when he was attacked by a mob and forced to defend himself and his subordinates. He was charged with murder and was rightly acquitted. On a general survey of the events of the last few years it must be admitted that respect for law and authority, which prevailed generally throughout India at the close of the nineteenth century, has suffered a notable set-back, and that the behaviour of the police in the face of sedulous temptation, calumny, boycott, intimidation, social ostracism and manifold efforts to undermine their loyalty, has been admirable. This staunchness on their part is the main reason why the almost continuous rioting of the years 1917-1922 did not develop into a greater catastrophe. It is to be hoped that the new legislative councils, introduced by the Montagu-Chelmsford Reform Scheme, will gradually show a keener appreciation of the efficiency and fidelity of the police. Up to the present, as the debates testify, they have given little active support to this first line of defence against anarchy, and on one or two occasions have shown towards the police a barely veiled hostility. It cannot be too often remembered that rioting is easily incited among huge masses of credulous and very illiterate people, such as are found in every province of India, and that once it starts on an appreciable scale, it rapidly gathers momentum and sweeps away all ordinary barriers of restraint. Stern and rapid repression of the first symptoms of general rioting and disorder, followed by expeditious action in the magisterial courts is the only adequate, and unquestionably the most merciful, method of combating the danger.

CHAPTER II

OFFENCES AGAINST THE PERSON

MURDER

ACCORDING to a popular saying in India, the three most potent causes of trouble and unhappiness in daily life are *Zan*, *Zar*, and *Zamin*, or 'woman, gold, and land.' This is particularly true of the crime of murder; for, if we exclude murders committed in the course of dacoity or rioting, the majority of the cases investigated by the police are directly traceable to relations between the sexes, disputes about land and village factions, and desire for gain. In any one year the motives underlying this crime may vary from province to province, and in some areas there are special reasons for taking life which do not exist elsewhere. But, generally speaking, one may ascribe to the three powerful stimuli above-mentioned most of the murders committed in districts as widely separated as the Panjab, Bombay, and Burma. In 1921, 735 cases of murder were recorded in the United Provinces; 697 in the Panjab; 719 in the North-West Frontier Province; 984 in the Madras Presidency; 309 in the Central Provinces; 84 in Assam; and 683 in Burma. In the preceding year 500 murders were committed in the Bombay Presidency and 200 in Behar and Orissa. In most instances the crime was directly due to sexual jealousy, agrarian disputes or hope of plunder.

Burma, which heads the list of all provinces in every form of serious crime except house-breaking and cognate offences, offered quite recently two striking examples of murders arising from factional hostility and sexual relations. The tenants of an estate in the Toungoo District were divided into two parties on the subject of rent-payments. A member of one faction reported to the police that one night his wife left the house for a few minutes for natural purposes, and that he was following her, to protect her against mishap, when they were both seized and bound by partisans of the hostile faction, and carried to a neighbouring temple. There the complainant was placed on one side of the shrine, and his wife on the other; and during the night, after the recitation of prayers, his wife was decapitated by one of their captors, while he was rendered unconscious by a blow on the neck from a *dah*. On recovering his senses in the morning, the complainant found himself alone with his murdered wife, and also discovered that some of her jewellery had been stolen and that his house had been burnt to the ground. The police, on visiting the temple, found the body of the unfortunate woman, with the head almost completely severed; while an examination of the complainant's injuries revealed eight parallel lines across the throat, which the medical authorities believed to be self-inflicted. The district police and the Criminal Investigation Department held an exhaustive inquiry, but failed to solve the mystery completely. They did, however, establish the fact that the woman had been murdered in her husband's house, which was straightway razed to the ground, in order to destroy incriminating evidence. The corpse was then placed in the temple, and a charge of murder was laid against several members of the hostile faction. The real object of this very heartless murder was probably the incrimination of the local 'die-hards', who declined to see eye to eye with the complainant and his party on the question of payment of rent.

The second case occurred in Thaton District. A Burman youth took a violent fancy to the adopted daughter of a villager, who acted literally as the household drudge. So hard-working and useful was she, that her adoptive father and his sons were determined not to lose her services, and put every possible obstacle in the path of the amorous youth. The latter thereupon abducted the maid and had his way with her, until the family, whose chattel she was, arrived in force and rescued her. Twice was the girl thus abducted and twice was she carried back again by force; and her owner then filed a complaint of abduction and rape against the youth and his friends. He failed, however, to substantiate the charges in court; and the lover, emboldened by the failure of the legal proceedings, thereupon appeared at the old man's house and demanded the restoration of his beloved. The home forces drove him and his supporters away from the house, and two of them followed the lover and slew him in full view of a large concourse of villagers. The police, who arrived promptly, recorded ample evidence of the murder; and on the statements of several eye-witnesses the two culprits were committed for trial. But the police had reckoned without the Law's delays. The interminable legal procedure, which is the curse of India and the despair of its police, afforded the old man and his sons ample opportunity to bribe the witnesses, and a local *pongyi* (priest), doubtless in return for 'value received', spent some time in actively destroying evidence. When the trial eventually took place, each witness in turn smilingly resiled from his or her original statement, and the police, after consulting the Government Prosecutor, were obliged to agree to a withdrawal of the prosecution. For an expenditure of a few hundred rupees, the old man thus secured the continuance of the girl's services and effectually silenced her passionate lover.

It happens not infrequently in India that deaths reported in the first instance as accidental or unnatural are discovered on inquiry to be cases of murder, and experienced officials can hardly be blamed for regarding with some suspicion the annual tale of deaths caused by wild animals or poisonous snakes. In Bengal, for example, in 1917, 35 cases of 'unnatural' death were subsequently proved to be murders; 14 similar instances occurred in Behar and Orissa in 1920, and 16 in Assam in 1921. In rural tracts it is often very difficult to decide whether a death, which may have occurred several days, or even weeks, previously, was caused by design, or, as reported, by accident.

Multiple or mass murders are not unknown, though they are naturally much less common than the murders of individuals. A shocking case occurred in the Betul District, Central Provinces, three years ago. An avaricious illegitimate son, determined to secure an inheritance, hired an assassin to kill his father and three legitimate half-brothers. The three sons were slain at night with an axe, while they lay asleep in a hut, and a stranger, who was also sleeping there, shared their fate. The father was murdered the following morning. The assassin was eventually arrested; but the crime could not be brought home to the man who hired him. Several double murders occurred in the Central Provinces in 1921, and in Drug a gang of aboriginal jungle-folk from a neighbouring Indian State robbed and murdered four travellers in a manner reminiscent of old *Thagi* days. Factional disputes were responsible for a tragedy in Ferozepore District in the same year. The village of Bareke was divided into two camps, which had carried on a protracted litigation in the local courts, ending in an appeal to the Privy Council. Exasperated by delay and other causes, one faction resolved to remove its opponents and their relatives once for all. Accordingly, its members, having mustered by night to the number of twenty, visited six houses in the village and brutally massacred eighteen people, including women and children. The litigation thus came to an abrupt termination, to the chagrin doubtless of the lawyers and pleaders, who were reaping a fair harvest from the litigious spirit of the village.

The two most sensational mass-murders of recent times were those at Nankana Sahib in the Panjab in 1921, and the massacre of twenty-two policemen at Chauri-Chaura, United Provinces, in 1922, both occurrences being in large measure the result of the lawlessness and disorder which were permitted to spread over India between 1917 and 1922. The tragedy at Nankana Sahib is instructive as an indication of what can happen in India when the Government fails to assert its responsibility for law and order. The fanatical 'reforming' Sikh party, having taken forcible possession of several Sikh shrines which enjoy large revenues, cast their eyes upon Nankana Sahib, sacred to the founder of the Sikh religion. The *Mahant* or Abbot of this wealthy shrine, having satisfied himself that the Panjab Government would not assist him in maintaining his position, decided to take his own measures for self-protection, and did so in a thoroughly Oriental fashion. The shrine is situated in a courtyard, surrounded by rooms facing inwards. The one entrance is guarded by a gate which can be closed. In these rooms round the courtyard the *Mahant* concealed his followers, loop-holing the walls for rifle-fire. A large body of 'reforming' Sikhs arrived at the shrine, apparently merely for worship and not with hostile intent; but when they were inside, the gate was closed, and they were then slaughtered wholesale by the *Mahant's* followers. This was followed by a great flame rising from the courtyard. The *Mahant* burnt the bodies of his victims with the help of oil purposely stored for the occasion. Out of about 200 Sikhs, only two wounded men escaped to tell the tale.

Among miscellaneous motives for murder, the blood-feud has peculiar importance in the Panjab and the North-West Frontier Province. Where sexual relations are involved, tribal custom in many places demands the death of the guilty party, and this fact partly accounts for the number of murders in 1921, 49 in the Panjab and 210 in the Frontier Province, which were directly traceable to blood-feuds. The general attitude of the Panjab public in these matters is illustrated by a case which occurred in the Hissar District three years ago. A man of lower caste had an intrigue with the wife of a Jat and murdered the husband, whom he found as much in his way as King David did the unfortunate Hittite. The police arrested the murderer and were escorting him to the police station, when they were attacked by a mob of Jats, who wrenched the prisoner from custody and beat him to death on the spot. Despite the open nature of the crime, evidence sufficient for a successful prosecution could not be secured. The blood-feud is of commoner occurrence in the Frontier Province and necessitates constant vigilance. A few years ago the local authorities tried the experiment of modifying the procedure in *jirga* trials, and settling on the basis of tribal custom disputes which had given rise to criminal offences. This involved a great reduction in the standard of penalties and corresponding relaxation of treatment. Needless to say, it proved quite unsuited to local conditions, and actually facilitated the commission of murder on easy terms. The number of murders due to blood-feuds immediately increased, showing that the Pathan is always ready to take advantage of the latitude allowed by the tribal code. The experiment was very properly relinquished.

As one might expect in a country 'marching in uneven stages through all the centuries from the fifth to the twentieth', feelings of revenge provide a strong stimulus to murder. Occasionally the victims are policemen or other lowly servants of the Government, who have aroused animosity by too faithful adherence to duty. In 1921 two constables were murdered in the United Provinces; in Madras, in the same year, two forest-guards were shot as they lay asleep, for having taken action against two villagers under the forest laws; and in Nellore a country-liquor contractor was killed, because he had been rash enough to appear as a witness for the prosecution in a case against some of Mr. Gandhi's non-violent non-co-operators. The murder of two constables by Adam Khel Afridis, as they were travelling by night along the Grand Trunk Road, may have been an act of revenge, but probably was intended as a reminder on the part of the tribesmen that police officers had much better spend their nights in the shelter of their stations. On the other hand, the villager in the Bombay Presidency who combined murder with arson, and succeeded in burning to death two women and some cattle in 1920, was certainly actuated by an uncomfortable desire for vengeance on their proprietor. The same may be said of the *bairagi* (wandering devotee) in Bengal, who murdered his mother in 1917, because she had driven his wife out of the house. He had probably more justification for his action than a villager in Bogra, who slew his mistress because she delayed unduly the preparation of his food. A little boy in the same province fared no better than the dilatory Aspasia, for he was poisoned because his brother had given evidence in a criminal case against the murderer. Vicarious punishment of this kind is well known in India. Feelings of revenge, coupled with exasperation at their non-success, prompted a gang of youths in Bengal to murder a young widow who had repulsed their advances; and private vengeance was certainly the motive in two cases in the North-West Frontier Province, in both of which a woman, unaided, murdered another woman whom she suspected of intriguing with her husband. One can hardly gauge the extent of the shock to the Western world, if this primitive form of retribution was suddenly adopted by neglected or jealous wives in European society.

A more subtle form of revenge, which is not uncommon in India, is the commission of murder with the object of implicating and throwing the blame upon another. The case of the murder of the woman in Burma, quoted in an earlier paragraph, is an instance in point; and another typical example occurred in Monghyr in 1920. An old man was murdered by his sons at the instigation of a villager, whose sole motive was to implicate a third party, with whom he was at loggerheads. It used to be said that for a hundred rupees or so one could purchase a murder in India, complete with corpse; and cases from time to time occur, which lend some colour to the assertion. But, as a rule, plots to secure the discomfiture or ruin of a rival or opponent stop short of the taking of innocent life.

Superstition, and the fear bred thereby, offer a powerful incentive to take life among the lower and less civilized castes or tribes. The witch and the wizard, with their potions, their spells, and their evil eye, are regarded with quite as much dread and abhorrence as they were in England in earlier days. The Province of Behar and Orissa reported eleven cases of murder of suspected witches or wizards in 1920, and the Indian Press from time to time notifies similar occurrences in other provinces. If not actually killed, the supposed witch is often subjected to grievous ill-treatment, for the average Indian villager, when driven by superstitious terror, knows no pity.

Many murders in India are due to miscellaneous causes and cannot be included in the main categories outlined above. Among such cases is that of the Chinese boy, aged seven, living in Rangoon, who refused, probably through ignorance, to relinquish his class name and take that of his adoptive father. Incensed at his apparent contumacy, the adoptive parents beat the boy unmercifully, burned his body with cheroot-ends, drove needles under his nails, and performed other abominable acts which cannot suitably be set forth in print. The case lends colour to the view that for sheer devilish cruelty there is no one to equal the Mongolian. Instances of 'running amok' are fairly common. A case occurred quite recently in the City of Bombay, in which a Muhammadan, engaged in prayer in a mosque, felt a sudden and imperative call, according to his own confession, to go forth and slay. He obeyed the summons to some purpose and stabbed several persons, including a police constable, before he was pluckily tackled by a Parsi resident and secured. In Jalaun, United Provinces, in 1921, a villager who had been dispossessed of his holding by the village headman, brooded over his wrongs until he literally 'saw red', and then proceeded to slay the headman and his own two daughters, and also tried to kill the headman's wife and his own wife. In Burma, if one may judge from a recent case in Maubin District, the vagaries of the man who 'runs amok' are regarded in much the same light as a cinema entertainment is by Western villagers. The culprit in this case, after severely assaulting several persons with a *dah*, murdered a friend and his wife in very brutal fashion. A crowd of about seven hundred people watched this 'dance of death', apparently unmoved, and made no effort whatever to seize the murderer. He would probably have accounted for several more victims, had not a sub-inspector of police rushed up and shot him dead in his tracks.

While sexual intrigue is responsible for many murders in India, 'lust-murder', as understood by Krafft-Ebing and other Continental students of sexual abnormality, does not, so far as is known, occur. The nearest approach to a sadistic murder of this type, perpetrated under overpowering sexual hyperaesthesia, occurred in 1910 in Bombay City, when a man, who was expert at climbing up the down-take pipes of lofty tenement buildings, murdered two women in succession—a Bania woman and a well-known flower-girl, after breaking into their rooms in the manner described and obtaining their favours. After his arrest he exhibited clear signs of being abnormal, and eventually died in the lunatic cells attached to the police hospital. True lust-murder, as one of the phenomena of *psychopathia sexualis*, appears to be better known in the more highly cultured countries of the West than in the East, where capital offences have their basis in less recondite mental processes.

In conclusion, it remains to mention the occurrence of murder in the guise of human sacrifice. Human sacrifice has prevailed widely in India in past centuries, and possibly was borrowed by the Hindus from the aboriginal tribes, whose primeval earth-gods and jungle goddesses could only renew their divine energy through the two-fold rites of the sacred marriage and the blood sacrifice. Mr. Rajendra Lala Mitra has shown that the custom of human sacrifice prevailed among the early Aryans, and India cannot claim freedom in later epochs from the stain of a practice which has been widely diffused throughout the world. Every student of customs and folklore in India is acquainted with the terrible *Meriah* sacrifices of the Khonds, which were suppressed by British officers between 1837 and 1854; and there is little doubt that the sheep, goats and fowls offered in these days to Kali, Durgadevi, Chamunda, and other savage goddesses of fertility, have taken the place of the human victims, whom it was once customary to sacrifice to these aboriginal deities. But although the sacrifice of human beings on the terrible scale prevalent in old days has long ceased, the practice is by no means wholly extinct in India. A case was reported among the Jats in the United Provinces in 1891; another case near Calcutta in 1892; and in 1902 an English magistrate in Ganjam received a petition for permission to perform a human sacrifice, intended to give a rich colour to the turmeric crop. A recent case occurred in Behar and Orissa in 1920, and another in Ganjam, Madras Presidency, in the following year. In the former a deaf and dumb beggar was sacrificed to an idol by a village priest and his son; in the latter a girl of four years was murdered in circumstances which showed clearly that her death was intended to appease a local goddess. Despite penal action, despite the introduction of 'responsible government', customs such as this die hard, and sporadic cases are likely to be reported for many years to come from tracts, in which the cult of terrific aboriginal gods and the promotion of fertility in men, animals and crops hold a predominant place in the mind of an ignorant and superstitious peasantry.

INFANTICIDE AND CHILD-MURDER

Thurston, in his *Ethnographical Notes in South India*, remarks that 'the sacrifice of infant life, so far as Southern India is concerned, may be classified under two heads: (*a*) Criminal offence, as a means of getting rid of inconvenient offspring or as an act of revenge; and (*b*) tribal custom.' This classification may be conveniently applied to the whole of India, subject to the proviso that female infanticide as a tribal custom is, if not extinct, at any rate comparatively rare. In discussing the latter phenomenon one must distinguish between two distinct types of tribal infanticide. Risley, in his *People of India*, pointed out that female infanticide of the savage kind was a direct consequence of exogamy, whereas among the Rajputs, who once enjoyed an unenviable reputation in this matter, it resulted from hypergamy. The former savage type has disappeared entirely from India. The latter, in Risley's opinion, might possibly exist in a modified or more subtle form; or, in other words, female life is less protected and less cared for at all ages, more especially in infancy, than that of males. In 1891 the general impression in the Panjab, where the practice had shown much vitality, was that female children were the victims of a certain amount of customary neglect which could not be styled intentional, but that in certain areas and among certain classes the evil assumed a more serious form, which might be illustrated by the couplet:

> 'Thou shalt not kill, but need'st not strive
> Officiously to keep alive.'

Twenty years later (1911) the India Census Report recorded the general view that, while it was very difficult to estimate the prevalence of female infanticide, the practice was on the whole comparatively rare. The same verdict is applicable to-day, the discontinuance of the practice on a noticeable scale being due for the most part to the labours of a succession of British officials. The late Dr. Vincent Smith, in one of his footnotes to the latest edition of Sleeman's *Rambles and Recollections*, recalled the severely inquisitorial measures adopted in Agra in 1870, while Colonel Willoughby's crusade among the Jharejas of Kathiawar prior to 1849 deserves to rank with the efforts of the officials who put an end to the practice of *Sati*.

But although wholesale female infanticide no longer exists, much carelessness in respect of female life still prevails. The absurdly heavy expense involved in the marriage of girls leads in some castes and classes to the birth of a daughter being looked upon as little short of a domestic calamity. The prevalence of such an idea side by side with vociferous demands for 'self-determination' and a growing national consciousness is possibly due, as Risley surmised, to the fact that the development of the literate classes in India has proceeded on irregular and one-sided lines, which tend to glorify intellectual and political ideals at the expense of the social and moral reforms which are essential to wholesome national life. But a light wind is stirring the dry bones of Hinduism. There are signs of a definite movement towards social reform and of a clearer recognition of the rôle which women can play in the future of India, and the day may yet come when such ideas as those underlying the neglect of female child life will be numbered among the memories of a vanished barbarism.

The practice of infanticide as a means of disposing of inconvenient offspring is more common in India than might be supposed from a perusal of official returns. Of such cases only a percentage finds its way into the police records, and the eight cases reported from Bengal in 1917, the eleven cases from Behar and Orissa in 1920, and the fourteen cases in the City of Bombay in 1921, probably represent but a small proportion of the number of infant-murders actually perpetrated. The object in nearly all cases is the avoidance of social disgrace. Their detection is usually difficult and, especially in large urban centres like Calcutta and Bombay, is rather a matter of luck than of patient investigation. The discovery of the dead bodies of newly-born or prematurely-born children in municipal refuse-carts and public latrines is not unknown in Bombay City, and their production before the medical authorities and final disposal are among the least attractive duties of the urban police force. The experience of other Indian cities is probably similar. The murder of children as an act of revenge is happily far less common, and when it does occur is more easily brought home to the culprit. An example was reported in 1921 in the Panjab, where a man deliberately murdered the infant son of a female hospital assistant, because his daughter had died while under her treatment. Revenge was the motive in the case quoted in an earlier paragraph, in which the brother of the murdered child had given evidence in a criminal prosecution.

Thurston, in the passage quoted above, makes no distinct reference to the ritual murder of children—a class of crime which once prevailed fairly widely, and still occurs sporadically in various parts of India. The practice, particularly in the case of male children, is based on a belief in the efficacy of the blood-sacrifice as a remedy for barrenness, and the culprits are therefore generally women. Sir Richard Temple has recorded, in Volume LII of the *Indian Antiquary*, the details of three cases which occurred in the Panjab and United Provinces during the closing years of the nineteenth century. Three fresh cases occurred in the Panjab in 1921; in all of them barren women murdered the children of neighbours, in the hope of thereby securing offspring of their own. In one instance the woman actually bathed in the murdered child's blood—an act curiously reminiscent of the charges made against the notorious Gilles de Retz in fifteenth-century France. This bath of blood is regarded in India as a supremely potent method either of exorcising the malignant spirits which prevent conception, or of securing the rebirth of the dead child in the womb of his murderess. The crime naturally occurs but rarely, and only among the lower and less civilized classes, whose mental and moral outlook has changed but little during the last hundred years.

Unnatural Offences

A certain number of cases of unnatural offence are heard annually in the Indian courts, but they are not sufficiently large to justify the view that homo-sexual or unnatural practices are particularly prevalent. On the other hand, such offences are difficult to detect and still more difficult to prove to the satisfaction of the courts, which wisely require that no shadow of doubt or ambiguity should attach to the evidence. Apart from this fact, the position of the police *vis-à-vis* of such offences suffers from the absence of any strong public opinion on the subject among the lower classes, some of whom do not appear to regard homo-sexual aberrations with the same repugnance as the upper and educated strata of Indian society. The accepted presence in some parts, e.g. Kathiawar and Bombay, of a recognized caste or class of eunuchs (*hijdas*) also tends to blunt the sense of disgust; for among some sections of the population these miserable anomalies, despite their propensities, are constantly summoned to sing songs and give rude performances of a very equivocal character on the occasion of domestic rejoicings, such as a birth or wedding ceremony. It is not easy to decide why on such occasions a repulsive-looking eunuch, dressed in women's clothes, should be preferred to the ordinary dancing-girl. The lower charges demanded by the former for their performance may be a factor in the case; but possibly an element of superstition also enters in, as the eunuch, being 'neither fish, flesh, fowl, nor good red herring', so to speak, is supposed on that account to be a more potent scarer of the malignant spirits that haunt such festivities as a birth-ceremony. Most provinces annually report a small number of cases of unnatural offence, e.g. 47 in Bengal in 1917, 19 in Assam in 1921. Calcutta recorded 12 cases in 1920. In Bombay, where few cases appear before the courts, the offence is sufficiently well known among the lower classes to have earned for those addicted to it an apt but unprintable sobriquet in the vernacular. Pederasty has usually been regarded as a peculiarly Muhammadan foible, and cases have occurred in Bombay, in which lower class Musalman women, desiring a divorce from their husbands, have not hesitated to accuse the latter before the *Kazi* of unnatural practices. Even if untrue or unaccepted by the *Kazi*, the charge is calculated to make the husband feel decidedly uncomfortable. The records of the courts and police, however, serve to indicate that the occasional commission of such offences is not confined to the Muhammadan community, and there is a suspicion that one or two at least of the young Hindu extremists of comparatively recent years, who paid the penalty for their crimes, were united by the bond of homo-sexuality. Considering India as a whole and the vast population inhabiting it, it is probable that unnatural offences and cognate practices are comparatively no more common, even in the capital cities, than they are in certain European countries.

Hurt; Rash Acts

It is perhaps hardly necessary to remark that cases of hurt, both grievous and simple, according to the definition in the Indian Penal Code, are of frequent occurrence in India, the annual number in some provinces running into four figures. Thus there were 2,663 cases of grievous hurt in the United Provinces in 1921, and 2,557 cases of simple hurt in Assam in the same year; Calcutta recorded 162 cases of grievous and 286 of simple hurt in 1920; while in the year following, Bombay City dealt with 272 and 273 cases respectively. A survey of several years' magisterial and other records would show a considerable variety of injuries inflicted and of methods employed to cause such injuries; but in a country which, at any rate up to a recent date, was for the most part disarmed and forbidden to possess or carry arms without a licence, the *lathi* or cudgel, usually made of bamboo and sometimes tipped with brass or iron, plays a prominent rôle in hurt cases. Among the *Goondas* of Calcutta and the *Mewalis* of Bombay, that is to say, among the hooligans and damaged characters of the less reputable quarters of both cities, are many individuals who can be hired to inflict injuries upon others; and when factional feeling runs high or sectarian animosity has been exacerbated, it is quite a common occurrence for one of the parties to hire one or more of these ruffians to waylay and assault his opponent. The practice of retaining a small bodyguard of such persons in permanent employ, which was once usual among Indian merchants, is now declining in Bombay, though it is still met with to some extent in Calcutta and other places; but the population of ruffianly hirelings shows no diminution on this account, and is not slow in times of popular disturbance to seize the opportunity of assaulting anyone it meets in the streets. The disgraceful riots in Bombay on the occasion of the visit of the Prince of Wales gave the *badmash* element an opportunity of attacking indiscriminately anyone, such as Europeans, Parsis and Native Christians, who wore Western dress, as well as many peaceable Hindus who had no sympathy with Mr. Gandhi's non-co-operation propaganda.

Another totally different form of hurt is caused by branding—a practice which, in the case of women and children, is based directly on the belief that this is the only efficacious method of driving out the devil which is supposed to possess them. Girls suffering from hysteria, children who appear to their relatives to be a little abnormal, are both liable to suffer in this way; for the lower and uneducated classes, who are firmly persuaded of the fact of spirit-possession and regard every disease as caused by malignant *bhuts* or *jinns*, pay no attention to Western theories of medicine and treatment. In some cases, however, branding is employed as a method of correction or revenge. This was the punishment meted out to a girl of tender years, who had drifted into a brothel and showed unwillingness to carry out the orders of the brothel-keeper, a very evil woman. The same method of inculcating obedience is sometimes employed by low-caste parents whose reverence for child-life is non-existent.

Rash and negligent acts involving criminal liability are frequently the result of gross stupidity, and occasionally meet with less punishment than they deserve. A curious instance happened a few years ago in Bombay. During the hot weather it is the common custom of residents in the central and crowded quarters of the city to sleep in the streets or in any available open space, owing to the intense heat in the squalid houses and *chals*. They lie in rows, each man or woman enveloped in a thin white covering, which shrouds them from head to foot; and as in most of the narrow streets and lanes nothing in the form of a footpath is provided, the people sleep literally in the street. A taxi-driver, returning late one night after discharging a fare, drove his car rapidly and without warning over four or five sleepers, some of whom sustained injury. He was very properly prosecuted by the police, who submitted that, considering the narrowness of the roads through which he was driving and the almost universal habit of using the public thoroughfares as dormitories, he was guilty of rashness and negligence, as well as of causing hurt in specific instances. The Indian magistrate, however, took a different view, holding that people who chose to sleep on the road instead of indoors were themselves rash and negligent, and, in fact, to use a vulgarism, were asking for trouble. He did not regard the taxi-driver as very much to blame for bumping over people who showed so little care of their own persons and so little appreciation of the primary and proper use of streets. The records of the Bombay magisterial courts also include a single instance, which occurred several years ago, of the prosecution of a builder and property-owner for rashness and negligence in the construction of a tenement-building. The house collapsed very soon after its erection, burying some of the inmates in the debris, and the police were able, after a prolonged and very detailed inquiry, to prove that the catastrophe was due to jerry-building of the most flagrant type. Considering the character of some of the private buildings erected in India, an occasional prosecution of this kind might be very salutary. But there are obvious difficulties in conducting such cases to a successful issue, while new municipal regulations and enhanced supervision have certainly been instrumental in preventing such criminally faulty construction as that which formed the subject of the Bombay case.

POISONING

Poisoning, as Crooke remarks in *Things Indian*, is a very ancient crime in India. The Law of Manu prescribed 'a fine for machination with poisonous roots, and for charms and witcheries intended to kill. A high-caste man was not to deal in poison, on pain of falling in seven days to the rank of a Vaisya or merchant.' Crooke quotes several notable historical instances of the crime, and relies upon a passage in Chevers' *Indian Medical Jurisprudence* to show that poisoning is not infrequent at the present day:

> 'The abundance in which a variety of deadly plants spring up in the hot and moist atmosphere of Bengal, and the unrestricted freedom with which nearly all the most potent kinds of mineral and vegetable poisons can be purchased in every Indian bazaar, added to the familiarity with the action of narcotics which has arisen from the daily habits of opium-eating and hemp-smoking, sufficiently account for the prevalence of the crime of secret poisoning among a timid people, who, except when wrought up to a state of frantic excitement, always prefer treachery to violence in the execution of their crimes.'

Since these words were written, the Indian legislature has passed an Act which considerably restricts the free sale and purchase of poisons, and it is no longer as easy as it used to be to obtain them in the bazaars. At the same time the use of poison in the commission of crime is still fairly common in India; and cases of road poisoning have occasionally been reported and serve as a reminder that the system of poisoning travellers, which was very prevalent after the forcible suppression of *Thagi*, has not been forgotten. In some cases, recorded in the later years of the last century, the criminals were proved to have belonged to families of Thag stranglers.

The number of cases in which stupefying drugs are administered, with the object of causing hurt or with the intention of facilitating the commission of theft and other offences, varies considerably by provinces. In 1921, for example, the United Provinces recorded 91 true cases; the Central Provinces, 68; the Punjab, 38; Madras, 23; Burma, 7; and the North-West Frontier Province, 4 cases. In the previous year there were 34 cases in the Bombay Presidency and 23 in Behar and Orissa. This form of crime occurs also in the large cities, and appears to be more prevalent in Calcutta than in Bombay, Madras and Rangoon. The poison generally used is dhatura or *stramonium*, which produces insensibility and delirium. Crooke ascribes the general familiarity of the people with this drug to the fact that, according to a native pharmacopoeia, dhatura, when mixed with a person's blood and smeared between the eyes, is a potent love-charm, and he quotes Dr. Chevers' belief that no drug known at the present day represents in its effects so close an approach to the system of slow poisoning, supposed to have prevailed in the middle ages. The use of pounded glass, as an irritant poison, is also not unknown. Diamond dust once enjoyed a still higher reputation; it was this substance, mixed with arsenic, with which Mulhar Rao, Gaekwar of Baroda, tried to poison Colonel Phayre, the Resident. Many of the reported cases of dhatura-poisoning occur within railway limits, and are committed for the purpose of facilitating robbery. Six cases were reported in the Rajputana Agency in 1920, in one of which a boy of eight years of age was waylaid by a Brahman and given some sweetmeats to eat. He immediately lost consciousness. The accused was arrested in due course; dhatura seeds and sugar were found concealed in his house; and subsequent inquiry proved that the culprit habitually practised this form of crime, selling his victims medicine to effect a cure, after he had poisoned them. In another case a constable, hearing a hue and cry, and seeing two men being pursued, managed to arrest one of them. It transpired that they had poisoned a Muhammadan with dhatura, and stolen his money. In the United Provinces, in 1921, some sweepers of Ambala, who had journeyed to Saharanpur to buy pigs, were drugged by some of their own caste fellows and robbed of their cash, and in Agra a notorious bad character was responsible for two cases, one of which ended in the death of a boy. In some of the districts of the United Provinces, e.g. Ghazipur, Bahraich and Gorakpur, this form of crime is distressingly frequent and is rarely detected. Seven professional poisoners, however, were arrested and convicted by the railway police in the United Provinces in 1921. Of these, one man had five previous convictions for poisoning to his credit. In every case their victims were drugged and robbed at railway stations.

CHAPTER III

OFFENCES AGAINST PROPERTY

Dacoity

Dacoity is the legal term used in British India for a system of robbery by gangs, and is derived from *daka parna*, meaning 'to plunder.' The dacoits of former days were robbers by profession, and brought up their children to the same occupation. Whitworth (*Anglo-Indian Dictionary*) describes them as banditti with strongholds to retire to, who committed raids on a large scale, their gangs often composed of several hundred men; and Balfour (*Cyclopaedia of India*) mentions among the former predatory races, who lived largely by dacoity, the Badak of the Nepal Terai, the Dasadh of Behar, the Nath, Ahir, Boria, Kurmi and Gujar. The Minas were concerned in most dacoities in Northern India, while in the south-west the Santal, with his club, long bamboo spear, and battle-axe, often swept down upon Birbhum, Hazaribagh and the adjacent districts. Nowadays the special significance of the term has become obsolete, and dacoity is used to mean any robbery carried out by a gang of not less than five persons, animated by a common intent. As a general rule, dacoity of the kind common in the districts of all provinces occurs but rarely in the large cities. The teeming population, the street-lighting, and the concentration of a police force in a comparatively limited area, militate against the success of the operation. A quite unusual series of daring dacoities was carried out in Bombay and its suburbs in 1921 by a gang of Baluchis, armed with fire-arms and other deadly weapons, who perpetrated two murders and injured several people with knives, *lathis* and hammers, before they were surrounded by the police. The gang had committed altogether 65 dacoities in Gujarat and the northern Konkan, and the police confiscated from the thirty-five persons composing it, four double-barrel guns, one smooth-bore, one revolver, three pistols, various other weapons, and much ammunition. The Report of Mr. Justice Rowlatt's Committee on Sedition in India, published in 1918, shows that Calcutta became painfully familiar between 1914 and 1917 with dacoities carried out for political motives. The constant immigration into that city of the members of regular criminal tribes, such as the Doms, Bhars, Palwan Dosadhs, Pasis, Kewats, and others, would itself constitute a menace to peace, were they not registered under Act III of 1911 and kept under more or less surveillance by the police. Of all the cities, Rangoon perhaps suffers most from dacoity. A serious increase in this form of crime, reported in 1921, was ascribed to the fact that the professional criminal is affected, quite as much as other classes, by the contempt for authority openly preached by professional agitators. In most of the cases the dacoits were armed with guns, revolvers and *dahs*, and launched their attacks in the heart of the town; and, owing to the difficulty of recognizing armed burglars, eight out of ten dacoities remained undetected.

The character of the ordinary dacoity, as committed outside the large centres of population, is well described in the Police Report of the United Provinces for 1921, which recorded 1,277 cases, due largely to political agitation and its resultant disturbances. Of this number, raiders from adjacent Indian States perpetrated 76; and more than 100 were committed by wandering tribes like the Bhantus, many of whom had escaped from criminal tribes settlements. The gang of dacoits appears suddenly without warning, locks up or disables the police, then loots the premises of a rich Bania, sometimes committing murder in the process. It then attacks a village, killing several of the villagers, if they defend themselves, and carries off all the loot it can find. In one instance an armed gang tortured a woman to death by burning; in two cases victims were strangled; in another case a woman and boy were killed with spears. One large gang of nearly 1,000 men literally emptied a village, causing a total loss of Rs. 40,000. In Bengal, as elsewhere, the main difficulty in dealing effectively with dacoity is lack of information. The list of known gangs in the possession of the police is a formidable one, and there are many actual and potential criminals about whom next to no information is available. The *chaukidar*, or village police officer, who is theoretically supposed to keep the regular force informed of all that happens in rural tracts, is generally useless; the public is apathetic and gives the police no help whatever; and the system of surveillance is quite unsuited to the conditions of the province. The officer in charge of a police station is expected to maintain surveillance, in addition to other multifarious and pressing duties, over an absurdly large number of criminals scattered over a wide area, destitute of proper communications and often inaccessible during certain seasons of the year. Any proposal made by the Government to remedy this state of affairs, by an increase of the force or other means, is apt to be angrily opposed by the politicians in the provincial legislatures. It is scarcely a matter of surprise, therefore, that gangs of Doms, Lodhas, Sonthals, Bhumij, and other professional or hereditary criminals, continue to levy a toll upon the countryside. The number of gangs registered for surveillance is constantly increasing; in one year about 48 gangs, comprising 4,041 members, were brought under the provisions of the Criminal Tribes Act in Bengal. The police struggle with the evil like Laocoon in the serpents' coils.

Conditions in Assam are very little better; for the professional criminal has taken advantage of the fact that during the last few years the police have been fully occupied in fighting the non-co-operation movement, and, as in other places, the public takes no steps to protect itself by giving the police information and assistance. Moreover, in Sylhet the problem of prevention and detection of crime is complicated by the geographical features of the district, which is seamed with rivers and tortuous *khals* (streams). The riparian villages of the main rivers are inhabited largely by criminals, who find a safe hiding-place in their inaccessible backwaters. Dacoity is also rife in Behar and Orissa, parts of which are liable to be plundered by criminal tribes from the Central Provinces or the territories of Indian princes. In 1920, 274 cases occurred, in many of which the police and villagers had to fight pitched battles with the gangs of marauders. In another instance, a police officer, having received news of the presence of a well-known band in the neighbourhood, decided to invite attack by disguising himself as a Bengali Babu and journeying in a *palki* (palanquin) through the jungle. The ruse was successful; the dacoits attacked in strength; and after a free fight one of them was arrested. A series of dacoities in the Palamau District was the work solely of the Korwas, an aboriginal tribe.

Uncivilized jungle tribes are equally troublesome in the Central Provinces. In 1921, two armed dacoities were perpetrated by Naths in Jubbulpore; on another occasion the police fought a regular engagement with a body of Korwas, armed with poisoned arrows; armed Bhils from Khandesh and Nimar attacked the houses of rich Marwadis in Buldana; a serious house-dacoity was traced to a composite gang of Pasis and other criminal tribesmen from another province; while a rapid series of six nocturnal attacks was the work of a band of Rohillas. As an indication of the connexion between crime and Gandhi's non-violent non-co-operation movement, it is interesting to record that the residents of one village, which had embraced the movement *con amore*, appointed as their village sub-inspector the head of a gang which had committed nine serious dacoities! Revolutionary propaganda and unrest led in some places to attempts to withhold the *baluta* (fees paid in kind for services performed for the village-community) due to the Mahars—a degraded tribe which serves as village-watchmen and scavengers. The Mahars naturally ceased to perform their duties, and in one tract sought a livelihood by resorting to predatory crime and incendiarism. The Madras Presidency recorded 880 cases of dacoity in 1921, exclusive of the serious outrages committed during the Mappilla rebellion in Malabar; and many of these crimes were committed by nomad gangs like the Padayachis in Arcot, the Donga Erukalas, who made descents upon Bellary, and the

Kallars from Madura, who chose Tanjore as the scene of their operations. Some idea of the burden of surveillance ordinarily falling on the Madras Police may be gathered from the statement officially published that the number of known depredators, receivers and suspects at large on December 31st, 1921, was 22,597.

Bombay suffers, like Madras, from the presence of a large number of predatory jungle tribes, among the most troublesome and the most impervious to civilizing influences being the Bedars (Berads) of the Southern Maratha country. The Bedars, who are identical with the Boyars of the Madras Presidency and have affinities with the Ramosis of the Deccan, have a long history of fighting and lawlessness. Many of them were employed in the army of Tipu Sultan, and some of their leaders were petty chieftains and *polygars* in the period preceding the establishment of British rule. Attempts have been made of recent years to group them in settlements and wean them gradually from their criminal habits ; but the bulk of the tribe still prefers to live by robbery under arms. One gang of them committed fourteen dacoities in the Belgaum District in 1921, before they were surrounded by the police and arrested after a sharp struggle.

In the Panjab and the North-West Frontier Province economic conditions have a distinct effect upon the volume of dacoity. When the crops are poor or fail, and prices rule high, this form of predatory crime usually increases. On the other hand, even in normal years many dacoities are committed by trans-border and trans-Indus offenders, most of whom carry fire-arms. In 1921, a gang of forty armed Pathans raided Hazro in Attock District, killed two constables and stole their muskets, and then looted seven shops and two private houses. Bands of outlaws from across the frontier caused similar trouble in the Frontier Province; they also kidnapped and held to ransom 185 people, including women and children. The more recent murder of Mrs. Ellis and the kidnapping of her daughter show the boldness with which these marauders operate and the great difficulties attendant upon attempts to rescue their victims. So far as concerns the Panjab, crime of this character has been steadily increasing since 1917; and although poor harvests and high prices have contributed to this result, there is little doubt that political unrest, involving a disregard of law and authority and distracting the police from their normal duty of watch and ward, has been mainly responsible for great daring on the part of the criminal. Constant vilification of the police, also, which is one of the salient features of the agitators' propaganda, has minimised their influence with the public, which is less ready than formerly to assist their investigations and preventive arrangements.

In Burma also, owing to certain constant factors, serious crime shows a marked upward tendency. Many of these factors are equally discernible in other countries, but are probably rendered more noticeable in Burma than elsewhere by the impressionable character of the Burman. 'Crime usually tends to be heavy wherever the cultivator has been divorced from a simple system of peasant proprietorship, wherever there is close contact with the material side of Western civilization, and where the growth of new desires has outstripped the acquisition of means to gratify them. In other words, the growth of crime in Burma may be part of the price which the country has to pay for her rapid development.' The Commissioner of a large district ascribes the present state of crime in Burma to various causes, such as (*a*) lack of parental discipline and the decay of moral and religious instruction, (*b*) the psychology of the Burman, (*c*) deterioration of moral influences, especially the Buddhist priesthood, (*d*) the system of discontinuous employment of labour, (*e*) the lack of public spirit, and (*f*) the careless attitude of the average villager towards violent crime. Be this as it may, the increase of dacoity in Burma is also ascribed to the political awakening of the masses by the modern indigenous politician. The young Burman villager hears the platform orator descant upon the iniquities of the existing Government, and is constantly exhorted to defy its authority and give proof of his independence. He cannot help remarking also the apparent immunity enjoyed by those who ceaselessly vilify the servants of the Government. This, doubtless, accounts for the fact, remarked by experienced police officials in Burma, that a new type of criminal, quite distinct from the criminal of past years, is now entering the arena.

Occasionally, however, dacoity appears to be prompted by a spirit of adventure, engendered by tales told by demobilised soldiers or by the exhibition of sensational cinema films. The difficulties of the police in coping with predatory crime in Burma are intensified by the almost incredible lack of public spirit and of courage in resisting malefactors. The tendency of villagers to accept the attacks of dacoits as merely an uncomfortable feature of the daily routine is well illustrated by a case reported in 1921, in which the whole village turned out and calmly watched five dacoits, armed with a home-made gun, which was fired by means of a lighted cheroot, help themselves to

10,000 rupees' worth of property and make a leisurely departure. In contrast with this apathy was the behaviour of a Burman girl, who, with her brother's help, pluckily cut down and captured two housebreakers.

There are one or two bright features, however, in this gloomy record of Burman criminality. Good work is being carried out under the Habitual Offenders Restriction Act, which aims at encouraging the criminal to adopt more reputable methods of livelihood. Among those reclaimed are a dacoit *boh*, who now works regularly as a carpenter; and a notorious dacoit, who is now flourishing as a physician, with a large and lucrative practice. He constantly appears before the Deputy Commissioner, in company with respectable householders, who ask that a permit be given to him to attend their relatives in Moulmein; and such requests are immediately granted. But the authorities have a heavy task before them to counteract effectively the addiction of the Burman to serious crime, committed under the influence of, or in the desire for, excitement.

Robbery

As with dacoity, economic conditions and the activity of regular criminal tribes affect to some extent the volume of cases of robbery in most provinces. A fair harvest, for example, in Behar and Orissa in 1920, coupled with the flourishing condition of the lac industry and successful police work against dacoits, was directly responsible for a decline in robberies in that province; whereas in parts of Bengal, two years before, increased resort to this form of crime was rightly ascribed to the partial failure of crops and unemployment. It is, indeed, a matter of common experience in Bengal, as well as in other parts of India, that scarcity due to failure of rain or to floods is usually followed by a distinct rise in the number of reported burglaries and robberies. Of the 101 robberies perpetrated in Calcutta in 1920, a large number were the work of bad characters from other districts, who were feeling the general rise in the cost of living; and the same conditions influenced the ordinary thieves and pickpockets, who, under the stress of high prices, commenced to adopt terrorist methods. The City of Bombay frequently experiences an outcrop of robberies, whenever famine conditions in Gujarat or the Deccan drive large numbers of hungry people to seek food and shelter in the urban area. The North-West Frontier Province tells the same tale. In 1921, for example, when the spring harvest failed, the local bad characters in Peshawar combined to form small gangs of footpads, who committed several highway robberies before they were finally rounded up by the police, while other robberies were the work of Powindah, Mahsud and Bhittani tribesmen, who suddenly swoop down from independent territory and are back across the border, before the local residents are aware of their depredations. In the United Provinces many highway robberies are committed by nomad criminal tribes, but occasionally sensational cases are perpetrated by individuals belonging to a higher social stratum. In the latter category can be placed two cases which occurred by daylight in the Civil Lines at Allahabad in 1921. In one case a man returning from the Imperial Bank in a hired *ekka* (carriage) was robbed of Rs. 10,000; in the other the culprits were two sepoys of the Sappers and Miners corps.

The value of property annually stolen in robbery, burglary, and theft cases is considerable, and the percentage of recovery varies from province to province. Thus in 1921 the value of property (in round figures) stolen and recovered was respectively, in Assam, 6·3 lakhs and one lakh; in Madras, 42 lakhs and 6 lakhs; in the United Provinces, 69·7 lakhs and 6·9 lakhs; in Rangoon, 3·3 lakhs and one lakh; and in Bombay City, 23·7 lakhs and 5·8 lakhs. The corresponding figures for the preceding year in Calcutta were 20·4 lakhs and 4·5 lakhs, and in the Bombay Presidency, including Sind, 25·2 lakhs and 8·6 lakhs; while in Bengal, in a fairly normal year, about 3 lakhs' worth of goods are recovered out of about 40 lakhs' worth reported stolen.

In many instances the police have no chance of recovering the stolen goods, owing to the time which elapses between the discovery of the loss and the report of the circumstances at the police station. This delay was particularly noticeable in the days of the plague epidemics, when people shut up their houses in the city through fear of infection, and spent two or three months of the hot weather in temporary huts at a distance from the town. Many robberies and thefts were committed in the empty houses, which were left inadequately guarded; but in most cases no complaint of loss was made to the police until the return of the owners, several weeks after the commission of the offence. In the large cities the regular criminal usually makes very complete arrangements for the rapid melting-down of silver goods and jewellery, and unless the loss is reported immediately, the chance of identifying the stolen property becomes remote. This is illustrated by a burglary which took place about midday from the bungalow of an English merchant, who happened at the time to be chairman of the local Chamber of Commerce. Most of his silver disappeared from the sideboard in the dining-room, including a handsome silver teapot of Indian workmanship. By a lucky chance the culprit was discovered and arrested four hours later, but all that remained of the property was several narrow bars of silver and a small silver elephant which had surmounted the lid of the tea-pot. In the dastardly murder of a rich Bhattia widow residing on Malabar Hill, Bombay, which occurred a few years ago, the heavy silver embroidery of her *saris*, as well as her silver and gold ornaments, had all been melted down within an hour or two of her death. Even so, they provided a link in the chain of evidence, which secured the conviction of the murderers.

BURGLARY

Burglary, house-breaking, lurking house-trespass and similar offences, occupy a prominent place in the criminal records of every province, and the volume of this class of crime fluctuates with economic conditions. The percentage of undetected cases is usually large, and indicates that the Indian burglar, unless he is caught red-handed, seldom meets with his deserts. For example, out of nearly 42,000 burglaries in Bengal in 1917, convictions were secured in only 1,291 cases. This result arises partly from a general lack of sympathy on the part of the public with law and authority, and partly from the fact that the sufferers often report that they have sustained no loss, being reluctant to face a prolonged investigation or to brook the interminable delays inseparable from legal proceedings in India. Latterly, also, complainants have shown a distinct apprehension of possible reprisals by the revolutionary organization which has engineered so many disturbances throughout the country. Scarcity is, nevertheless, the predisposing cause of burglary. It was responsible for a large proportion of the 18,000 cases reported in the Panjab in 1921, and for most of the 1,637 cases in the North-West Frontier Province in the same year. The Peshawar cantonment, which once suffered from constant burglaries, has now acquired considerable immunity, owing to a much-needed increase of constabulary, the provision of barbed-wire entanglements, better street-lighting, and an improvement in the behaviour of the Afridi tribes. On the other hand, the 54,000 burglaries, which occurred in the United Provinces in 1921, are ascribed to the general unrest caused by revolutionary political propaganda, coupled with the difficulty of using effectively the preventive sections of the Criminal Procedure Code and with the lack of time available to the police for the work of surveillance and patrol duty. The figures of burglaries for the same year in the Central Provinces and Madras were respectively (in round figures) 20,000 and 11,500. A large number of cases occur annually in Behar and Orissa, and between 7,000 and 10,000 in the Bombay Presidency, while Assam and Burma escape comparatively lightly with 5,000 and 6,000 cases. These figures, however, are liable to considerable fluctuations owing to special temporary causes, such as industrial or agricultural depression. Statistics published in the Police Report of the Bombay Presidency for the year 1920 indicate that in England and Wales reported crime, both serious and ordinary, is proportionately heavier per *mille* of population than in the Bombay Presidency (and some other provinces), but that in respect of violent crime and burglaries Bombay has a decidedly heavier percentage. The incidence per *mille* of population of serious crime, calculated by provinces for the year 1919, was as follows:

Central Provinces, 4·61; Burma, 4·49; North-West Frontier, 2·87; United Provinces, 2·68; Bombay, 2·37; Bengal, 1·99: Assam, 1·92; Behar and Orissa, 1·89; Panjab, 1·80; Madras, 1·59.

Ordinary burglary in rural areas is not, as a rule, remarkable for ingenuity; but in the large cities house-breaking has been elevated to a fine art. Some burglars are adept at disguising themselves; others, who prefer to operate practically naked, smear their bodies with oil, which renders difficult their seizure and retention by a wakeful householder. Much use is made by burglars in some cities of the filthy sweeper's *gali* (passage), which separates one house from another and is intended solely for the use of the *halalkhor*, and occasionally a burglar has been known to make good his escape by wriggling through the privy on the ground floor. A belief was prevalent in old times (it is mentioned by Dr. John Fryer in his *New Account of East India and Persia*, 1675) that Indian burglars scaled houses by holding on to the prehensile tail of the *ghorpad* or iguana, and the surname of a well-known Brahman family in western India is derived from a tradition that one of its ancestors scaled an impregnable fortress in this manner. Nowadays Indian burglars prefer to attain proficiency in climbing up the water-pipes of high buildings, and some of them can by this means raise themselves to the fourth and fifth storey of a dwelling-house. Occasionally one meets with a master mind among burglars—a man who can plan, direct and execute his operations with real care and ingenuity. Such a man was the Parsi, Nanabhai, who defied the Bombay City Police for nearly twenty years, and during that period carried out a long series of clever burglaries. He organized a perfect system of assistance and espionage, paid liberally both those who assisted his operations and those who might inform against him, and was eventually arrested red-handed by the merest chance. The heavy bribes which he offered to his captors to connive at his escape from custody, and which unquestionably he could have paid, proved that for him burglary had been a most paying profession.

THEFT

The annual number of thefts is naturally large in a country which contains so many nomad castes and tribes, whose hereditary occupation is crime, and such a vast illiterate population, whose standard of living and whose wants have increased more rapidly than their wage-earning abilities and opportunities. Some provinces record as many as 25,000 and 30,000 cases of ordinary theft in a year, and under the most favourable conditions the number hardly falls below 5,000 or 6,000. The proportion of convictions to recorded complaints is not high; for detection is often impossible, while want of public spirit, the imperfect presentation of cases in court, the cleverness of many criminals, the law's delays, and the practice of tampering with witnesses, combine to prevent the success of the prosecution. Thus, in Bengal in 1917 the total number of thefts recorded was nearly 23,000, but convictions were obtained in only 4,200 cases. The class of property stolen ranges over the whole gamut of personal possessions, from currency notes and hard cash to agricultural produce, telegraph wire, bicycles and firearms. Thefts of arms are rightly regarded as of peculiar importance in India, and are of frequent occurrence. Five revolvers were stolen from the shop of a licensed dealer in Bombay in 1911, five days before the arrival of Their Majesties the King and Queen in India, but were fortunately recovered by an excellent piece of detective work on the part of the C.I.D. In 1921, the Panjab reported constant thefts of revolvers as well as of Government arms and ammunition from the Arsenal at Ferozepore. The latter were perpetrated mainly by convicts employed as extra labourers in the Arsenal. Thefts of rifles from British regiments are fairly frequent in the North-West Frontier Province, and tribesmen are occasionally arrested in possession of the stolen arms. Two Ut Khels were thus arrested in 1921 with six Government rifles stolen from a British regiment at Fyzabad. Rangoon criminals appear to be able to obtain revolvers without much difficulty, most of them being weapons that have been surreptitiously imported. In past years the carelessness of Europeans and others, in legal possession of revolvers, has facilitated their abstraction by domestic servants and others, who can always sell them for a fair price in the bazar. Perhaps the most sensational case on record was the theft of Mauser pistols from Messrs. Rodda and Co., a firm of gunmakers in Calcutta, during the course of the Bengal anarchist conspiracy. In August, 1914, the clerk of Messrs. Rodda and Co., whose duty it was to clear imports of arms and ammunition at the customs office, had cleared 202 cases of arms, etc., but had brought only 192 cases to his employers' warehouse in Vansittart Row. He had then left, saying that he was going to bring the remainder. He never returned, and after three days the matter was reported to the police. The ten missing cases contained 50 Mauser pistols and 46,000 rounds of ammunition for them. Of these weapons, 44 were distributed almost immediately to nine different revolutionary groups in Bengal, and it is certain that these pistols were used in fifty-four cases of dacoity or murder, or attempts at dacoity and murder, which occurred after August, 1914. By 1918 the Bengal Police had succeeded in recovering thirty-one of these stolen pistols in various parts of Bengal.

Another special form of theft takes place from railway premises and from running trains. So far all attempts have failed to check effectively this class of crime, which is committed daily with impunity. In many cases, as in that of the big railway-yards at Asansol in Bengal, the thieves are railway employés, and any attempt to grapple with the evil is apt to be frustrated by departmental friction. Thefts from running trains form the bulk of railway crime in the Central Provinces, and in Behar and Orissa, which in 1920 recorded more than 4,000 cases of theft of goods in transit. Little improvement can be expected until the railway companies provide themselves with a really effective watch and ward system. No province can show a clean sheet in respect of thefts from railways, and the trouble is as constant and serious in western and southern India as it is in the northern and eastern provinces. The amount of pilfering which takes place from goods yards and transit platforms is little short of appalling. The Railway Police Committee discovered that the total value of property stolen on Indian railways amounts to at least one million sterling every year. The Panjab suffers so greatly from this form of crime that in 1921 special measures were devised to cope with it. 'Armed observation patrols were placed on selected night goods trains. When thieves were seen to board the train, signals were made to the engine, the train was stopped, and the police jumped out to grapple with the offenders. Often the signal was not observed, and the police very pluckily jumped off the running train at the risk of serious injury. In some parts of the province it was not merely a question of tackling well-defined gangs. Every village along the line was ready to turn out with axes, *lathis* and hammers to loot goods trains, whenever an opportunity presented itself. There were several encounters between the police and looters, in which two constables were wounded, and six thieves were killed and twenty-three were wounded.' These thefts would be rendered practically impossible, if the railway companies took to fastening all wagon doors securely by means of rivets or some similar device.

In Rangoon special attention has to be paid to thefts of rice, which are the work of organized gangs of thieves. These organizations, whose depredations amount to as many as 100 to 500 bags of rice a day, have been carrying on a systematic swindle for years. Both in Rangoon and in other capital cities an epidemic of thefts takes place at intervals in the European residential area, these thefts being mostly committed by day, and generally at hours when the owner is absent at his office and his servants are indulging in their afternoon siesta. A long series of thefts of this type was perpetrated a few years ago on Malabar Hill, Bombay, by a young Borah, who was at length pursued and arrested. He was sentenced, on conviction, to a short term of rigorous imprisonment, and on his release from jail recommenced his operations in the same area. But jail-life had blunted his faculties and diminished his agility; for he was easily caught while committing his fourth theft, and received a sentence which put an end to his activities for a long term of years. An amusing case occurred in

Rangoon in 1921. There had been many thefts from the quarters of the Royal Scots, until one day a young Madrasi servant was discovered in one of the rooms. To the officer who seized him he presented a printed card, which stated that the bearer was deaf and dumb and subsisted on the charity of the public, who were asked to support him. He feigned deaf-mutism extremely well, and begged alms of the officer by signs. The officer, however, handed him over to the police, who, feeling suspicious about his apparent infirmity, sent him to the hospital, by pre-arrangement with the police surgeon, under the pretence of having an operation performed on his tongue. The prisoner still persisted in his pretence; and it was only when the surgeon caught hold of his tongue and pretended to cut it with a knife, that he gave up the game and spoke fluently.

CATTLE-THEFT

Cattle-theft stands in a class by itself and is a widely prevalent form of crime, except in the North-West Frontier Province, where it occurs to an appreciable extent only in the Dera Ismail Khan District. The returns of cattle-theft, supplied by the various provinces, are admittedly no true index of its prevalence, as many cases are never reported. In some places, e.g. Behar and Orissa, the people are so afraid of reprisals that they report the cattle as 'strayed', while in Bengal the sufferer usually prefers to pay blackmail, as a surer method of recovering his property than the average police inquiry. As a rule, the cattle are returned directly the money is paid. In Burma, the increased cost of living is stated to be chiefly responsible for the three or four thousand cases reported during the year; but cattle-theft undoubtedly offers that element of excitement for which the Burman apparently craves. This craving for adventurous freebooting supplies the motive as often as not, while the apathy of the average villager prevents this form of crime from becoming unduly hazardous to its perpetrators. An instance may be quoted from a report by the Deputy Commissioner, Meiktila. Fifteen cattle were stolen from a village, were driven twelve miles across country, and were kept for four days before the owners traced the surviving animals. Five of the animals were butchered one by one by the thieves, the beef being sold and eaten publicly. Yet practically no evidence was forthcoming of any of these facts, and the police were unable to elicit sufficient information to justify prosecution of the offenders. In Lower Burma there exists a skilfully organized system of cattle-lifting, the animals being passed from hand to hand and from district to district so rapidly that detection is practically impossible.

Fraud and Cheating, Misappropriation, Criminal Breach of Trust, etc., etc.

Of the methods of obtaining money and goods by swindling, fraud and misrepresentation, India offers innumerable examples; and while many of the cases differ little in character from similar offences in Europe, a certain number depend for their success upon the ignorance and superstition of the peasantry, and are on that account less common among more educated and civilized peoples. To the latter class belongs a case which occurred at Hoshangabad, in the Central Provinces, in 1921. A Chamar (tanner), finding himself short of money, persuaded certain villagers to accompany him by night to a lonely temple in the jungle, where he undertook to double their jewellery, if laid out upon a stone. The dupes agreed. But no sooner was the jewellery placed on the stone, than one of the Chamar's accomplices appeared in the darkness, clad in appropriate disguise, and cried, '*Bhut! Bhut!*' (i.e., 'goblin'). The villagers thereupon fled in terror from the shrine, and the jewellery was 'spirited' away. The Non-Co-operation movement, initiated by Mr. Gandhi, offered many chances of profiting by the excessive credulity of the illiterate masses. In Bilaspur, for example, some local *kasais* (Muhammadan butchers) toured the countryside, spreading a story that Gandhi had issued orders that all goats were to be set free after the *Dasahra* festival. Having thus established a thorough slump in the goat-market, they proceeded to buy heavily, acquiring a large quantity of live stock at very low rates. In Behar and Orissa, in 1920, an imaginative individual cheated many persons by alleging that the suits won by the Bettiah Raj for enhanced rent had been upset by a new law, promulgated by Mr. Gandhi and Mr. C. R. Das, the Bengali agitator, and that he had been appointed *Kanungo* (surveyor) to make the necessary alterations in the survey-registers on payment of Rs. 5-12 for each correction. He had collected a considerable sum of money before the police were informed of his proceedings and put an end to his career. During the prevalence of the rumours disseminated by agitators that Gandhi's 'government' had superseded British rule, a man in Assam, who pretended to be an agent of Gandhi, made a good profit by selling white pills to the coolies of a tea-garden as an antidote to the poison, which he declared the English manager of the garden had mixed with the water of the garden wells.

Frauds upon insurance companies in respect of cotton are common in Bombay. A case occurred in

1920, in which a gang of swindlers, posing as cotton merchants, hired a ginning press up-country, insured a quantity of non-existent cotton for 1½ lakh, and then, having procured a moderate quantity of cotton for their immediate purpose, proceeded to set fire to it and claim the full sum from the companies concerned. Rumours of fraud, however, reached the ears of the companies, the police were called in, and the culprits received their deserts. The huge cotton-fires, which have from time to time caused a scandal at the old Colaba cotton-green in Bombay, were undoubtedly fraudulent in origin, despite attempts to ascribe their outbreak to spontaneous combustion. Often it was found that the cotton had been fraudulently mixed or that it had been insured for more than it was worth; and in certain states of the market it obviously paid the cotton-merchant better to defraud the insurance companies by burning his goods than to hold on to stocks which had been misdescribed and miscalculated. A thorough examination of the books of various native companies, which was carried out by the Bombay Police in 1914, established beyond any doubt that considerable fortunes had been made over the conflagrations by those in the cotton trade, as a result of fraud in the dealing, mixing, and classification of cotton. Clever underwriting, coupled with negligent methods of insurance, facilitated these frauds, and the immunity of the culprits was practically guaranteed by the constant refusal of the insurance companies to lay a formal complaint to the police and support a prosecution.

The following are a few illustrations of various forms of cheating and swindling, taken at random from the annual police reports of the provinces. A sub-inspector of schools at Saran, in Behar and Orissa, systematically defrauded the District Board by forwarding recommendations for bogus stipends. The Board remitted the stipends by postal money-orders, of which the sub-inspector's accomplices took delivery. A Syrian Christian, in Madras City, obtained delivery of various telegraphic money-orders by means of bogus telegrams, and the directors of the 'Madras Hindu Permanent Fund' played a very ingenious fraud upon the public by means of bogus cheques. A bogus charity institution in Bombay made considerable profits by exploiting charitably-disposed merchants, before a limit was put to its activity in 1916; a forged cheque for Rs. 50,000 was the means employed by four Bengalis in Calcutta to defraud a local bank in 1920. In the same city the 'confidence-trick' was performed with much success among middle-class and poor people, by a woman, posing as a wealthy heiress, and two male accomplices; while another gang posed as cooly *sardars* and reaped a fair harvest by undertaking to provide cooly labour in return for advances of money. Two interesting cases were reported in the United Provinces in 1921. In the first a professional swindler duped a vakil (High Court pleader) by pretending that he could secure for him an appointment as Deputy Collector, and actually sent him a forged letter of appointment, purporting to have been written by the Chief Secretary to Government. In the second case some petty local officials in Ghazipur induced a large number of unsuspecting villagers to join them in purchasing War Loan cash certificates. They subsequently misappropriated the money thus collected. In the Panjab in the same year some booking-clerks of the North-Western Railway carried on a fraud for some months by selling old tickets to passengers. Bundles of such tickets, numbering several thousands, were recovered after the fraud had come to light. The loss caused to the railway company may be roughly gauged from the fact that within two months after the discovery of the offence, the takings of the railway increased by Rs. 30,000.

Calcutta and Bombay were both interested in a bogus sweepstake and lottery promoter, belonging to the former city, who was arrested in Bombay in 1915. Muhammad Khan, to give him his proper name, for he had several *aliases*, had at different times promoted the following swindling concerns: 'The Pioneer Commission and General Supplying Agency, Bombay', the handbills of which bore the legend, 'Honesty is the best policy'; 'The Union Hall Grand National Sweepstake of 1914'; 'The Health Medicine Society'; and 'The St. Leger and Lincolnshire Cup Sweepstake'. He used to divide his time between Calcutta and Chandernagore, in order to float his concerns with a minimum of risk, and had already been once convicted by the French courts in the latter city of running a bogus lottery. Bombay City took early steps in 1914 to deport an Austrian, who suddenly appeared in the European quarter, and set up as a medical practitioner with the rank of honorary captain. This man persuaded several European foreigners to let him treat them medically for a heavy fee. Some of his patients suffered severely in consequence, and one of them nearly died as a result of his unskilled ministrations. The police entertained more than a suspicion that the pseudo-physician was actively interested in the illicit cocaine traffic.

The European loafer, who has sometimes served in the British Army, figures in several cheating cases. A member of this confraternity, who represented himself to be an officer of the R.A., but was afterwards proved to be a deserter from the Army, ordered stores to the value of Rs. 2,600 from several merchants in Bombay. He instructed the latter to send the stores to a certain station up-country, nominally for the use of a regimental institute; and some of the goods were actually despatched. Fortunately, the bogus officer was suspected and arrested before he had time to leave Bombay and take delivery of the stores at their destination. At the time of arrest, the accused was dressed in the uniform of a lieutenant, R.F.A. The police investigation showed that he had deserted from a British cavalry regiment in 1910, that he had six previous convictions for fraud, and that he had also perpetrated several swindles in other parts of India, which had not been proved against him. A more disgraceful case was that of 'Captain Harrison', an ex-officer of a British cavalry regiment, who systematically defrauded a French prostitute, with whom he had formed an acquaintance in Madras, after his release from a term of imprisonment. Having deprived the unfortunate woman of all her money, Harrison sent her to a brothel in Bombay and lived on her earnings. The police prosecuted him on three charges of cheating, and secured his conviction.

A curious case of fraud, in which there was an element of comedy, occurred in 1913. A Bania merchant, aged 60, was extremely anxious to marry again, but found that, by reason of his age, no family of his own caste was willing to give him one of their daughters in wedlock. This made him very despondent. His delight may therefore be imagined, when three Hindus approached him and, representing one of their number to be a Bania, offered him this man's sister, aged nine years, as a bride.

The Bania was in an ecstasy, and willingly consented to pay the trio a sum of Rs. 1,500 for the privilege of wedding the nine-year-old virgin. The marriage was hurried on. But, alas! the intimacy of the wedding night shattered his hopes and dreams. The girl was not a Bania, but belonged to a much lower caste, and he realised that he had been defrauded into contracting a flagrant *mésalliance*. A wave of anger drove him to seek the assistance of the police, who arrested the three matchmakers and succeeded in securing the conviction of two of them. What ultimately happened to the bride is not known, but probably she was not sorry to bid adieu to a bridegroom, who, as Indian marriages go, was almost old enough to be her great-grandfather.

Criminal breach of trust is a common form of crime in India; and among the clerks and other employés of Indian business firms it often originates in the unrestrained speculation and gambling which flourish in urban centres. Government departments also are not immune from this offence. One of the stipendiary police courts suffered a loss of Rs. 2,000 at the hands of a Native Christian clerk a few years ago, and in 1914 a Hindu clerk in the Government Law School in Bombay was charged with misappropriating Rs. 1,000, representing the fees paid by law students during a period of twelve months. The police inquiry also proved that between 1902 and 1912 the same clerk had embezzled more than Rs. 12,000. A charge of criminal breach of trust as a carrier was successfully sustained against a bullock-cart driver, who loaded his cart with bales of cotton piece-goods valued at Rs. 2,500, and handed them over, by previous arrangement, to a gang of accomplices, all of whom were Marwadi piece-goods merchants. An interesting example of criminal breach of trust by a servant was recorded in 1918. An Indian merchant in Bombay entrusted his servant, Rajaram, with two cheques for an aggregate sum of Rs. 40,000, instructing him to cash them at a local bank and bring back the money. Rajaram did not return; and the merchant in some alarm telephoned to the bank, which informed him that the cheques had been cashed. An immediate complaint to the police resulted in the arrest the same evening of Rajaram, who declared that he had been taken ill on the road, while returning with the money, and had been robbed of the whole amount as he lay half-conscious on the ground. The police were unable to disprove his story, and the case remained for the time being undetected. Two years afterwards (August, 1920), however, the police received news that Rajaram's family, residing in the Allahabad District, U.P., had redeemed an old mortgage on a village and had actually purchased two other villages. This was *prima facie* so unusual that a further investigation was made, which ended in the arrest of Rajaram and his brother, a full confession of their guilt, and the recovery of a large portion of the money which Rajaram had misappropriated two years before.

Shortly before the outbreak of the War (1914-18) India became unfortunately familiar with cases of criminal breach of trust by bankers. A serious instance occurred in the Panjab, and four prosecutions took place in Bombay. The most notorious of the Bombay cases—the collapse of the Indian Specie Bank—was, under the instructions of the Local Government and in accordance with views expressed in the High Court, never brought before a criminal court. The Directors, however, were known to have been very negligent of their duties, while the manager of the bank, who had been trying to make a 'corner' in silver with the depositors' money, found it convenient, when the crash occurred, to die suddenly at his residence in Bandora. It was generally held that he had committed suicide—and the circumstances were certainly suspicious—but further inquiry was silenced by a death certificate, signed by two Indian medical men, to the effect that his demise was due to natural causes. In three of the four cases placed before the courts convictions were obtained, falsification of accounts and the issue of false balance-sheets being clearly proved in each case. Prosecutions undertaken in other parts of India were equally successful, and the disclosures elicited at the trials of the offenders shattered public confidence for the time being in these mushroom financial concerns.

MISCHIEF

One of the commonest forms of mischief in India is the poisoning of cattle, and the prevalence of the offence may be partly gauged from the fact that at the Census of India in 1901 a number of persons were described in the schedules and enumeration-sheets as 'cattle-poisoner' by occupation, and were ultimately classified with 'prostitutes' and others under the main category of 'unproductive labour'. The Chamars, according to Crooke (*Things Indian*), often poison cattle for the sake of their hides, by administering arsenic in a ball of sugar, which they place in the animal's feeding-trough. Another method is to form a paste from the seeds of the *Rati* (*abrus precatorius*) and apply it to a sore or gall in the skin. The seeds, used raw in this way, furnish an active poison. The annual returns of cattle-poisoning in the various provinces are quite untrustworthy and give no real indication of the prevalence of the offence; for people who have suffered the loss of their beasts are often deterred by fear of reprisals from making a complaint to the police, and they are also reluctant to embark upon criminal proceedings involving much loss of time and money and constant appearance in a distant magisterial court. It is open to question whether the western system of criminal procedure and the law of evidence, which England has imposed upon India, are wholly suitable for the more primitive tracts. From the standpoint of the villager it must sometimes appear wiser to bide one's time and take one's own measures of reprisal than to submit to a lengthy police investigation and a protracted hearing in a law court. Allied to cattle-poisoning is the cruel practice of flaying cattle and other domestic animals alive. Here also, the number of such offences annually recorded gives no true estimate of the prevalence of this form of mischief. Four cases were reported in 1921 in the United Provinces; in the previous year 17 goats and a heifer were flayed alive in Behar and Orissa. The practice is not likely to be relinquished, so long as the magisterial courts impose small fines of Rs. 10 and Rs. 15 on conviction, as has been done in Behar.

Incendiarism is another common form of mischief, and has been deplorably frequent during the political unrest of the last few years. In 1921 the Central Provinces recorded 965 cases of mischief, in many of which shops, e.g., liquor-shops, were burnt as the result of the Non-Co-operation propaganda. Similarly, during the protracted industrial disturbances in Madras, which were the direct consequence of seditious agitation, there were many instances of wilful incendiarism, and on one or more occasions the humble dwellings of the low caste workers, who were generally opposed to the strike, were destroyed wholesale. Grave disturbances in all parts of India are generally accompanied by incendiarism. At the *Muharram* riots of 1908 in Bombay, for example, the Pathans, who live on the fringe of the Muhammadan quarter, began setting fire to shops on Parel Road and threw an unfortunate police constable into the middle of the flames. Incendiarism was a salient feature of the grave outbreak at Ahmedabad in 1919, at Chauri-Chaura, and other places. As a rule the proportion of detected cases of mischief is not large; for even where moral conviction as to culpability exists, it is often impossible to secure sufficient legal proof of the commission of the offence. Bengal, for example, in 1917 recorded only 1,238 convictions out of a total of 17,333 cases of mischief. From time to time these offences are the work of lunatics or persons of unsound mind, like the young Christian convert, who in 1921 set fire to the ceremonial cars belonging to Hindu temples in four districts of the Madras Presidency.

CHAPTER IV

PROSTITUTION IN INDIA

HISTORICAL ASPECT OF PROSTITUTION

DR. W. CROOKE, in an article on 'Indian Prostitution' in Hastings' *Encyclopædia of Religion and Ethics*, has remarked that 'at the present day prostitutes are tolerated in India to an extent which can hardly be paralleled in any other part of the world.' Of recent years a certain number of educated Indians, who have imbibed western ideas and education, have openly dissociated themselves from practices of long standing, which tend to popularize the prostitute's profession; but their number is very small by comparison with the total population of the country, and it is hardly an exaggeration to say that the great majority of India's inhabitants, representing orthodox and conservative opinion, still regard the profession, and those who follow it, with tolerance, and sometimes even with respect and approval. The cause of this phenomenon must be sought in the dual sphere of history and religion, which, in the popular guise of tradition and superstition, exercise a profound influence upon Indian life, and result in social anachronisms, which strangers view with amazement and are unable to understand.

Prostitution has existed in India from time immemorial. Crooke points to passages in the *Rig Veda* which demonstrate its existence in the Vedic age, while the Buddhist *Jatakas*, which were compiled about 350-300 B.C., prove that courtesans were tolerated and commanded a certain amount of respect at that epoch.

The fees paid to them were high; as many as 700 were housed in the palace of a king. We hear of a famous courtesan of Ujjayini, Devadatta, who lived in a sumptuous house; Ambapata, the famous *hetaira* of Visala, figures in Buddhist legend; the Princess Salavati actually adopted the prostitute's calling. It is fairly obvious that at this early date the prostitute and the courtesan occupied a recognized position in the social scale.

During the period of the Mauryan Empire, founded by Chandragupta (325-298 B.C.), the courtesan and prostitute occupied a privileged position at the royal court and actually co-operated with one of the most important departments of the imperial administration. Their position is defined in the famous *Arthasastra* of Kautilya, Chandragupta's Brahman minister, who is supposed to have compiled this great treatise on state-craft between 321 and 300 B.C. In chapter xi, it is stated that 'Prostitutes shall do the duty of bathroom servants, shampooers, bedroom attendants, washerwomen and garland makers. When presenting to the king water, scents, fragrant powders, dress and garlands, servants, accompanied by the above-mentioned prostitutes, shall first touch these things with their eyes, arms and breasts.' A later chapter (xxvii), headed, 'The Superintendent of Prostitutes', deals in detail with the duties and liabilities of these women. Those who were noted for beauty, youth and accomplishments were appointed to the king's court on a high salary, and were divided into three classes, according to their good looks and the value of their jewellery. It was their privilege to hold the royal umbrella, the golden pitcher, and the fan, and to accompany the king when he sat on the throne or was borne in his litter or chariot. A prostitute had to commence her musical performances at court at the age of eight, and she could only regain her liberty by payment of a heavy ransom: when she grew old and ugly, a post was found for her in the royal storehouses or kitchen, or she was appointed a nurse (*matrika*). The Superintendent of Prostitutes fixed the earnings, expenditure and inheritance of every prostitute; she was bound to give him accurate information of her daily fees and of her probable income, and also to disclose the name of her paramour. The Mauryan Government levied from each woman the earnings of two days in the month, or between six and seven per cent. of her income at least. A woman who preferred to live with an individual paramour and ceased to attend the court, had to pay a monthly sum to the Government, and could not dispose of her jewellery and other property without paying a fine. If, in contravention of royal orders, she refused to yield her person to anyone, she was punished with flogging and fine; if she was guilty of hurt or defamation, she was liable to various penalties; and if she murdered a lover, she was burnt to death or drowned.

In addition to their ceremonial duties at court, the prostitutes of the city and camp were members of one of the most efficient and extensive secret services that India has ever known. 'That service was worked very much on the lines followed by the German Government before the War, and with an equal absence of scruple. The king employed hosts of spies or detectives, masquerading in disguises of all kinds, who were controlled by an espionage bureau. The doctrine of the need for constant espionage in every branch of the administration pervades the whole of the *Arthasastra*, which treats every form of villainy as legitimate when employed in the business of the State.' The Greek writer, Strabo, records that professional prostitutes co-operated with the royal spies and were a recognized medium of intelligence. 'They must', writes Dr. V. A. Smith, 'have transmitted at times to their masters strange packets of scandalous gossip.' The practice survives to this day in an attenuated form; and though in British India the courtesan is no longer officially recognised and honoured, the police do not wholly disdain the information which such a woman is sometimes able to supply in regard to crime and popular movements.

Coming to the early centuries of the Christian era, we find definite reference to prostitution in the *Institutes of Manu* (*c.* 200 B.C.-A.D. 200), 'the moral textbook of the orthodox Hindu'; and various sidelights upon the position of the courtesan in the *Kama Sutra* of Vatsyayana, written about A.D. 250-300, which may be described as the Indian *Ars Amoris.* Many of the ideas in the latter treatise on Erotics seem to have been borrowed from older works, as, for example, the *Sutras* of 600-200 B.C. and the *Atharva Veda*, which contains several passages dealing with love-charms and philtres. It is also known that prior to the date of Vatsyayana, Babravya had compiled a voluminous work on the same subject, and that a treatise on one section of his work was written by Dattaka at the request of the courtesans of Pataliputra, the capital of the Mauryan Empire. The result of this literary activity, coupled with the system followed at the royal court, was that the science of Erotics had been placed on an equal footing with the sciences of *Dharma* and *Artha* as a branch of learning that Indian princes had to acquire (H. C. Chakladar, in *Journal Behar and Orissa Res. Soc.*, June,

1919). The *Kama Sutra*, which probably dates from the second half of the third century A.D., deals in minute detail with the position, customs, classification, behaviour and daily life of public women, and proves beyond doubt that skilled courtesans occupied from the earliest times an important position in Indian society. Occasionally they gave large sums for charitable and other public purposes. An inscription of the Western Chalukya dynasty of Badami, dating from the early years of the eighth century A.D., records donations by a prostitute to a temple.

The records of later ages indicate that public women still occupied a recognized position in the social economy, and further that the system of setting apart definite quarters of the city or town for their occupation had become stereotyped. This arrangement, which persists in India to the present day, was unquestionably followed in the Mauryan age, and contemporary evidence shows that it was the salient feature of the State control of prostitution in the Vijayanagar Empire (A.D. 1336-1646). Domingo Paes, the Portuguese traveller, who visited Vijayanagar in 1522, states that the women attached to the temples—

> 'are of loose character and live in the best streets in the city. It is the same in all their cities; their streets have the best rows of houses. They are very much esteemed, and are classed among those honoured ones who are the mistresses of the captains. Any respectable man may go to their houses without any blame attaching thereto. These women (are allowed) even to enter the presence of the wives of the king, and they stay with them, and eat betel with them, a thing which no other person may do, no matter what his rank may be.'

Abdul Razzak, who visited Vijayanagar as Persian envoy in A.D. 1443, during the reign of Deva Raya II, tells the same tale. 'Opposite the mint', he writes, 'is the office of the Prefect of the City, to which it is said 12,000 policemen are attached; and their pay, which equals each day 12,000 *fanams*, is derived from the proceeds of the brothels. The splendour of these houses, the beauty of the heart-ravishers, their blandishments and ogles, are beyond all description. It is best to be brief on the matter.' Some of the women were very wealthy; one of them was reported to possess 100,000 pieces of gold. Considering that prostitution was an acceptable source of revenue to the Government, and that the police force was paid out of the women's earnings, it was perhaps as well, from the standpoint of the Hindu administration, that the women should make considerable profits. The official and public recognition of prostitution, in vogue at Vijayanagar, characterized other governments in southern India in the fifteenth and sixteenth centuries. Some people are apt to assume that it is only during British rule that public women have been confined to recognized areas in Indian cities. The evidence of historical records shows that the system dates back to an early age, and south Indian inscriptions prove clearly that as early as A.D. 1004 the great temple of the Chola king, Rajaraja, at Tanjore, had attached to it 400 women, who lived in free quarters in the four streets contiguous to the shrine.

Prostitution was equally recognized under Muhammadan rule, though with occasional exceptions the Government did not treat it as a source of public revenue. Tavernier draws a striking picture of the position in the Golkonda kingdom (A.D. 1512-1687), and alludes to the public recognition of the women by the king.

During the reign of Akbar, according to the *Ain-i-Akbari*, prostitutes at the capital were so many that they defied enumeration. They had a separate quarter of the city assigned to them, which was known as 'Shaitanpura' (translated 'Devilsville' by Crooke); a *darogah* (overseer) and a clerk were appointed for it, who registered the names of all those who visited prostitutes, or who wanted to take any of them to their houses. Provided the tax-collectors were informed of it, people might indulge in such connexions; but they were not permitted, without sanction, to take dancing-girls to their own homes. If any courtier wished to have a virgin, he had in the first instance to apply for permission to the emperor. During Shah Jahan's reign, great liberty was given to public women, 'of whom the greater number were dancers and singers. All of them paid taxes to the king' (Manucci, *Storia do Mogor*). Aurangzeb, at the beginning of his reign, left matters *in statu quo*, but later he ordered that all prostitutes must marry or leave his dominions. 'This was the cause', says Manucci, 'that the palaces and great enclosures in which they dwelt went to ruin little by little: for some of them married and others went away, or at least concealed themselves.' He also remarks that, although Aurangzeb placed a ban upon music, he continued to entertain dancing and singing women in his palace, for the diversion of his queens and daughters. He conferred special names on their 'mistresses' or superintendents, such as 'Light of the Eyes', 'Seraphic', 'Lady of Paradise' and 'Freckles'. 'All these women', writes the Italian chronicler, 'are pretty, have a good style and much grace in their gait, are very free in their talk and exceedingly lascivious, their only occupation, outside the duties of their office, being lewdness.'

Dancing-girls and courtesans were an indispensable accessory of the confederate Maratha states. Sivaji alone forbade women, female slaves, or dancing-girls to accompany his army on active service. Any soldier discovered to be keeping one of these women was liable to be beheaded. Sivaji, however, kept concubines himself, and had no objection to public women taking part in ceremonials. Jasvant Rao Holkar had dancing-girls attached to his camp; for on one occasion he had a captured British soldier strangled and decapitated, and made the women dance round the head, stuck on a spear, for the amusement of himself and his entourage. Broughton speaks of the gift of nautch girls to Daulat Rao Sindia by the Jaipur ruler, and adds that in Sindia's camp 'Nautch girls are exempted from all taxes, though they pay a kind of voluntary one monthly to a *fakir*, who remains in their quarter of the camp, their several proportions being adjusted according to the strength of the set and the vogue in which its female members may be at the time of payment.' Most of the Peshwas followed the time-honoured custom, particularly Baji Rao II, whose court was more gay and licentious than that of his predecessors.

The evidence set forth in the preceding paragraphs indicates that from a very early date prostitutes occupied a recognized position in society, lived in quarters specially set apart for them, were granted honorary positions at court, and represented an important source of State revenue. Although the recognition of prostitution as a source of public revenue seems to have fallen into desuetude from the reign of Aurangzeb, the courtesan and prostitute continued till comparatively recent times to occupy a privileged position and were treated with no little respect. The example thus set by former

Indian governments and princes probably accounts in part for the tolerance with which prostitution is regarded by a large body of conservative opinion in India.

Religious Aspect of Prostitution

In his *Adonis, Attis, Osiris*, Sir James Frazer has discussed at length the subject of religious prostitution, and traces its connexion with the worship of a great mother goddess, personifying all the reproductive energies of Nature. It is probable that the prevalence of sacred prostitution in India, which survives to the present day, is likewise based upon the cult of the Dravidian earth-mothers or mother-goddesses. This mother-goddess, whose worship in northern India is largely in the hands of women, needed to be periodically refreshed with human blood, whence arose the sacrificial practices of the Khonds and other non-Aryan peoples. The fertility of the soil depended also upon the periodical marriage of the mother-goddess with a male consort. The cult of this divine pair is found in varying forms all over India, and supplies the basis of the sanctified harlotry in vogue at some of the larger shrines. The sacred prostitutes attached to the temples were perhaps regarded as the wives of the god, and in their licentious intercourse they imitated the licentious conduct of the mother-goddess, for the express purpose of ensuring the fruitfulness of fields and trees, and of man and beast.

Sacred prostitutes in India are known by the names of *Devadasi* or *Devaratial* ('servant of God'), *Kudikkar* ('those who belong to the house') in Travancore, *Murli* ('a flute') in the Deccan and Bombay and *Basavi*, *Bhavin*, *Devali*, or *Naikin* in the southern districts of western India. Although the system of religious prostitution is of great antiquity, the caste of temple-women seems to have first risen to prominence about the ninth or tenth centuries A.D., 'during which much activity prevailed in southern India in building temples and elaborating the services held in them' (Hastings' *Encyclopædia*). Reference has already been made to the 400 women belonging to the great temple at Tanjore in A.D. 1004. Tavernier describes a temple, about six miles from Cambay, which most of the courtesans in India used to visit. 'When the old courtesans', he writes, 'have amassed a sum of money in their youth, they buy with it young slaves, to whom they teach dancing and lascivious songs, and all the tricks of their infamous trade. When these young girls have reached the age of eleven or twelve years, their mistresses take them to this pagoda, and they believe that it will be good fortune to them to be offered and abandoned to this idol.' The Abbé Dubois, who describes the *Devadasis* of south India at the close of the eighteenth century, states that every temple of any importance had in its service a band of eight, twelve or more, and that these were bound to grant their favours to anybody on payment. Their official duties consisted in dancing and singing within the temple twice a day, and also at all public ceremonies, their songs being chiefly obscene descriptions of some licentious episode in the history of their gods. These women also accompanied persons of distinction, when the latter were paying formal visits to their friends, and they also attended marriages and other solemn family meetings. They were the only women in India, who enjoyed the privilege of learning to read, dance and sing, and as they drew only a small fixed salary for their duties at the temple, they supplemented it by selling their favours as profitably as possible. At the beginning of the nineteenth century there were 100 girls attached to the temple at Conjeeveram; and even to-day at Madura, Tanjore and Conjeeveram, there are numbers who receive allowances out of the large temple endowments. Moor, when he visited Khandoba's temple at Jejuri, near Poona, in 1792, found more than 200 sacred harlots, some of whom were very handsome: and despite the fact that the dedication of minor girls to temples is an offence under the penal law of British India, the number of *Murlis* dedicated to the god Khandoba is still considerable.

The chief duties of the *Devadasis* and other sacred prostitutes have always been to dance in the temple, to fan the idol with Tibetan ox-tails, to sing and dance before the god, when carried in procession, and to carry the sacred light styled *Kumbarti*. In Travancore they also fast in connexion with the temple festivals. The *Bhavin* of the Deccan has to sweep and purify the temple floor, while the male members of the caste, who are styled *Devalis*, blow the temple horns to wake the god from his slumbers. A *Devadasi* is regarded by the lower classes as a bearer of good luck, because she can never become a widow. Hence she is often deputed to walk at the head of Hindu marriage processions, instead of an ordinary married woman, who, being liable to widowhood, is not proof against evil omens met on the road. Her *tali* (neck ornament) is also regarded as lucky; and some Hindus send the *tali* required for a forthcoming marriage to a *Devadasi*, who prepares the string for it and threads on it beads from her own necklet. Among the Are Dammaras of Madras, a caste of acrobats, the marriage badge is actually tied round the bride's neck by a *Basavi*, or sacred prostitute, and the marriage ceremonies are supervised by a superannuated harlot of the same class. In the Bellary District a caste of harlots, known as *Madiga Basavis*, play a very prominent part at the festival of the village-goddess Uramma. In former days a *Kalavant*, or prostitute, figured as one of the recognized servants of the old village-communities of the Deccan, and, like the others, was granted rent-free land or payments in cash or in kind, in return for her services. The *Murlis* of Khandoba in these days often leave the temple at Jejuri, and, forming a troupe with two or more males similarly dedicated to that god, wander about the villages and towns, singing erotic songs and giving rude performances of a more or less licentious character. They often visit Bombay, where they enjoy a certain popularity among the lower classes, and have occasionally given performances which had to be prohibited by the police. The lower classes believe that the *Murli* is possessed at times by the shadow of the god, and on such occasions they consult her as a soothsayer and lay money at her feet.

These sacred prostitutes form a regular caste, having its own laws of inheritance, its own customs and rules of etiquette, and its own caste councils to see that these are observed. The act of dedication usually consists in marrying the girl to the idol or god, or to some inanimate object like a sword or dagger, the *tali* or necklet symbolizing marriage being tied round her neck by a male member of the caste. The caste is recruited in various ways. Sometimes the women themselves choose one or more of their children to succeed them as temple servants; others dedicate themselves, or are dedicated by their parents and relatives, in pursuance of vows made to the god; others again adopt female children with the object of dedicating them to the temple service.

In Marwar there exists a class of prostitutes known as *Bhagtin*, i.e. the wife of a *Bhagat* or holy man. Among these women it is necessary for a girl to be nominally married before commencing her career of prostitution, and a mock marriage is arranged between the girl and a *sadhu* (religious mendicant), who is always prepared to relinquish every connexion with his bride for a small payment of 1½ rupee. If no *sadhu* can be found, the ceremony of *phera*, or circumambulation of the portrait of the Hindu god Ganesh, is performed instead. Buchanan, quoted by Sir James Frazer, records the fact that in the Tulu-speaking districts of south India any woman of the higher castes, who wearied of her husband, or as a widow grew tired of celibacy, might go to a temple and eat the rice offered to the idol. Thereupon, if she was a Brahman, she had the right to live either in the temple or outside: but if she lived in the temple, she had to perform the usual duties there, and had to confine her amours to the Brahmans. The male children of these women formed a special class, called *Sthanikas*, while the daughters were either brought up to their mother's profession, or were married to the *Sthanikas*. Those women who preferred to live outside the temple had to pay a fixed sum annually to the temple funds.

Further evidence of the system of religious prostitution observed at various Hindu temples is available in literary works and official records. But enough has perhaps been adduced to justify the view that superstitions connected with the widely-prevalent worship of fertility-gods and mother-goddesses must have helped to confirm the Indian attitude of tolerance towards prostitution, referred to at the opening of this chaper. Church and State, indeed, seem to have combined to popularize, if not to honour, the prostitute's profession; and with the example of their governments and the teaching of the priesthood before them, it is hardly surprising that the general mass of the people of India should have learned to regard the trade of the courtesan and prostitute with considerable tolerance, and in some cases as almost worthy of respect.

Modern Prostitution

Side by side with the sanctified harlotry described in the preceding paragraphs, there has for ages existed ordinary prostitution of a commercial type, more nearly resembling the evil as it exists in western countries. Up to the date of the abolition of the Contagious Diseases Act, the Indian Government exercised a certain ineffective supervision over prostitution, and could give an approximate estimate of the numbers employed in the trade. But the repeal of that Act and the practical impossibility of differentiating between professional and clandestine prostitutes are together responsible for the absence of reliable statistics of the present number of public women. At the decennial census of 1911 prostitutes were curiously included in the major class of 'unproductive labour', together with beggars, vagrants, habitual receivers of stolen goods, and cattle-poisoners. It is, perhaps, hardly necessary to remark that the statistics are far from trustworthy.

Prostitution, as it exists in India to-day, falls under the two main heads of (*a*) indigenous or Indian prostitution and (*b*) European prostitution, which has gradually developed in the maritime cities of India since the opening of the Suez Canal in 1869. As regards prostitution among Indian women, one must differentiate between those who, as already stated, embrace the profession in accordance with the dictates of religious belief and custom, and those who follow it as a regular business or means of livelihood. In northern India the latter are known by various names, such as *tawaif*, *patar* (Sk. *patra*, an actor), *kanchani* (golden), *randi* (widow), *kasbi* (Arab. *kasb*, acquiring); while those who practise the trade secretly are called *khanagi* ('those of the house') or *harjai* (gadabout). They are often recruited from widows, or women who have been expelled from their caste for misconduct (Crooke, in Hastings' *Encyclopædia*). Many gipsy-like nomadic tribes in northern India prostitute their girls as a matter of custom. The Bediyas, for example, reserve nearly all their girls for prostitution, and the men of the tribe keep concubines drawn from other castes. In some places, if a man marries a girl of the tribe he is expelled, and if he marries a girl who has been reserved for prostitution, he is fined by the caste-council. The Kolhatis (wandering acrobats) of Bombay depend largely on the prostitution of their women, and a Kolhati girl, on attaining puberty, is allowed to choose between marriage and harlotry. If she chooses the latter, she appears before the caste-assembly, and with the consent of its members becomes a prostitute. The tribe has been known to kidnap high-caste girls, in order to bring them up as harlots, and is therefore kept under police supervision. The custom of prostituting their girls is also followed by the Harnis, the Berads or Bedars, and the Mang Garudas who are generally speaking, professional robbers and thieves. The Dombars (acrobat caste) of Mysore are notorious for dedicating their smart and good-looking girls as prostitutes, and one girl out of every troupe is always reserved for this trade. The initiation takes place when the girl comes of age, at the temple of Anjaneya or Yellamma, a regular ceremony being performed, in which rice is poured over her by *Basavis* and married women, while she sits on a rice-pounder in the midst of her caste-people. In the same State the Beda, Golla, Kuruba, Madiga and other castes often dedicate their eldest daughter, if no son has been born, and similarly a girl who falls ill is vowed to a life of celibacy, with the usual result (Crooke, *ibid.*).

In Behar and the adjoining districts of the United Provinces there is a certain Naik caste, the women of which frequently become prostitutes (*tawaif*) and are much in request for dancing and concubinage. They are permitted by caste rules to prostitute themselves only with men of the higher Hindu castes, and are forbidden to consort with non-Hindus. Another caste rule obliges them to confine their favours to one man for one night. The son of one of these women, if asked for his father's name in a court of law or elsewhere, invariably gives his mother's name in reply. In western India many women of the Dhed caste of Gujarat and of the Mhar tribe of the Deccan become common prostitutes, and will be found in the lowest class of brothels in Bombay City. Both the Mhars and the Dheds are degraded castes, the Mhars in particular having acted from time immemorial as the watchmen and scavengers of the walled villages of the Deccan. A good many Mhar women are dedicated to Khandoba, and become *Murlis* or sacred harlots, like the women of the Maratha Kunbi class ; but a much larger number embrace the prostitute's profession merely for the sake of a living. Women belonging to some of the higher classes, e.g. Vani and Marwadi, will also be found serving in the large cities ; but these cases are fewer in number, and such immorality as exists in these classes is clandestinely practised, as a rule, with selected paramours.' In Bombay, and possibly also in Calcutta, there are houses and rooms occupied exclusively by Japanese women, by Jewesses from Baghdad, and by Arab prostitutes. The Japanese, who have brought with them to India the habits of the *Yoshiwara*, formed a powerful attraction to the Gurkha regiments at the time of the departure of the expeditionary forces for France (August, 1914); and the sectional police had much ado to keep order and settle disturbances in the particular street where these women mostly reside. The brothels are generally managed by a *souteneur*, whose ostensible business is that of tattooing. The traffic in Arab prostitutes, which is in the hands of Arab procuresses, is often marked by great cruelty. In 1911 the Turkish Consul in Bombay requested the police to help in repatriating some of these unforunates, and in consequence of the inquiry that ensued, one Arab brothel-keeper was deported and several girls were sent back to their homes in Baghdad. One of the girls was discovered to be quite insane, though it could not be ascertained whether this was due to ill-treatment or other causes.

In northern India prostitutes often live in brothels managed by a procuress, who treats her customers to tobacco and to various compounds of opium and hemp. Both Hindu and Musalman recruits for the trade are obtained from among the illegitimate children of courtesans, or from female children adopted by prostitutes, and also by purchase from agents, who travel through Central India, Rajputana, and other districts, picking up unwanted girls of tender age for a small sum, sometimes as little as Rs. 5 or Rs. 10, and then selling them at a profit to brothel-keepers in the larger towns and cities. A good many children are deliberately kidnapped, and it is open to question whether the annual return of cases recorded or investigated by the police is any true index of the total amount of kidnapping. The Panjab recorded 349 cases in 1921; the United Provinces, 370 cases; Burma, 253 cases; Madras, 103 cases; the Central Provinces, 90 cases; Behar and Orissa, 79 cases; and Assam, 23 cases. Traffic in women is rife in the Panjab. In 1921 a regular sale depôt was discovered in the Hissar District, and a large number of women were found in wrongful confinement. They belonged to various castes and hailed from different parts of the country. In Hoshiarpur, Ludhiana and Ambala there is also a regular trade in women, who are hawked from place to place by professional cheats. 'Very few cases come to light,' writes the Inspector-General of Police, 'because the women are often content with their lot!' In some districts of the United Provinces there is a definite traffic in girls with the Panjab, while Allahabad and Banda contain local matrimonial agencies, whose methods are not always above suspicion. But the professional kidnapper probably finds a more convenient field for the exercise of his activities in the territories of Indian States.

On the other hand, female life is held extraordinarily cheap among the lower classes in India, and the birth of a daughter is apt to be regarded rather as a domestic calamity. Cases not infrequently occur in which young girls are abandoned by their relatives, who find themselves unable to provide the money required for their betrothal and marriage, and these little 'derelicts' sometimes find their way into brothels, where they are fed, clothed, and taught singing and dancing until they reach puberty, when the brothel-keeper arranges to sell their first favours for a good round sum to some well-to-do townsman. Muhammadan prostitutes, who are numerous throughout India and range from the inmate of a low-class brothel to the wealthy courtesan, who earns a high fee for her singing, occupies well-furnished quarters, and drives in her own motor-car or carriage, are recruited in the same way. In a case, which happened a few years ago, a poor Muhammadan in the Madras Presidency, having borrowed money at a high rate of interest to provide dowries for his two elder daughters, and being unable to raise a further sum for his third daughter's marriage, sold her outright to a brothel-keeper for Rs. 40. The girl was about eight years old when she entered the brothel, and by the age of thirteen she was helping to support her unnatural father and two young brothers out of her earnings as a prostitute.

Respectable people, both European and Indian, are usually shocked by the sight of the lower-class prostitutes who, in the streets of some cities, sit behind bars, like caged animals, in rooms opening directly upon the street. In Bombay one well-known thoroughfare is notorious in this respect. It is not always understood, however, that the bars are put up, not for the purpose of what has been styled 'exhibitionism' in reference to the *Yoshiwara* of Japan, but to save the women inside from being overwhelmed by a low-class rabble, ready for violence on the smallest provocation. A few years ago, before the women placed bars in front of their rooms, there were constant scenes of disorder, resulting occasionally in injuries to the women; and it was on the advice of the local police authorities that the women had the barrier erected, which obliges their low-class *clientèle* to form a queue outside and enables the women to let in one customer at a time. Considering that a prostitute of this class charges only four annas for her favours, it is not surprising that disease is extremely common, and that the offering of fourpence to Venus results, a few days later, in a further expenditure on the quack remedies of some local Æsculapius. Complaints are also made against the system of allowing prostitutes to occupy whole streets, it being supposed that if they were evicted and scattered over the town, the evil would be less apparent and therefore less revolting. But in India it is the traditional and established custom of each class and community to reside, as far as possible, in its own particular quarter. Differences of caste, creed and custom render this arrangement inevitable. Secondly, the practice of segregating prostitutes in a special portion of the urban area is really a legacy of the system established by preceding Hindu and Moslem governments. Occasionally in past years local authorities have taken action to remove public women from a particular locality, in response to public feeling on the subject. But the result has not been wholly satisfactory, as the women spread themselves over a larger area and settle down in streets previously respectable, to the natural annoyance of the older residents. Little help in this matter can be expected from the average Indian landlord, for he usually charges a prostitute a higher rent than he can obtain from ordinary tenants, and he insists upon being paid his rent monthly in advance.

Of recent years Indian opinion has shown increased sensitiveness in the matter of public prostitution, and appears desirous of restricting purely commercialized vice. Private Bills on the matter have been presented to the Indian legislature, and India has been represented at the conferences dealing with the traffic in women and children, which have been held at Geneva under the ægis of the League of Nations, and has actually assented to the fixing of the age of consent at 21, despite the fact that most Indian girls mature at the age of eleven or twelve years and even earlier, and commence cohabitation before they reach the age of fourteen. How the Indian politician and legislator will contrive to co-ordinate this decision as to the age of consent with the circumstances of religious prostitution and hereditary harlotry, sanctioned by the Hindu caste system, remains to be seen. If orthodox and conservative opinion takes the same stand that it did a few years ago, when the age of consent was the subject of legislation, there is likely to be considerable opposition to action based upon the more advanced age accepted by the League of Nations.

Apart from this question, however, much might be done by practical effort to diminish the immoral traffic in children in India, although the difficulties which face the reformer are by no means trivial. Few institutions exist to which rescued children can be consigned, and in the case of Hindu girls caste-prejudices and caste-customs are productive of serious complications. This difficulty disappears in the case of Muhammadan girls, and there is at least one orphanage in India, which feeds, clothes and protects stray Moslem girls, and, when they reach maturity, arranges for their regular marriage with men of their own faith. This institution was founded in Bombay by a former Commissioner of Police. The same city contains an orphanage for Hindu girls; but, as it receives children of the upper classes only, it can offer no protection to Sudra and out-caste children, who are more exposed to debauchery than the children of more favoured sects and communities. There are possibly similar homes in Calcutta. But the public mind has still to be stirred out of its habitual nonchalance in regard to prostitution, and its ancient disposition to regard female child life as of less value and importance than that of male children. And when it is widely recognized by the people of India that the daughter of the Mhar or the Mang Garuda has as much right to protection as the daughter of the Brahman or the Vani, and that the trade of the public prostitute, whether carried on in the darker quarters of an Oriental city or in the shadow of some aboriginal deity's shrine, is not a delectable calling, then one may expect the imposition of a real check upon the activities of the procurer and procuress, who batten upon the immoral traffic in lost or unwanted children. As exemplifying the recognition of the prostitute as an integral feature of society, the advertisement of a native performance, which was widely distributed in the form of handbills a few years ago in Bombay, is reproduced *verbatim* as an Appendix to this book.

Turning to the subject of European prostitution in India, which is frequently misdescribed as the 'White Slave Traffic', it may be stated at the outset that the women who ply the trade are found only in the chief maritime cities, namely, Calcutta, Bombay, Madras, Rangoon and Karachi, and are chiefly of Russian or Eastern European nationality. Their total number is not large, and it decreased after the outbreak of war in 1914, owing to the deportation at the end of that year of such of them as belonged to countries at war with Great Britain, and to the check imposed by war conditions upon fresh immigration to India. Women of this class usually come to India of their own free will, after serving an apprenticeship in Europe, Constantinople or Egypt; and although they are usually in debt when they arrive, and remain so for the rest of their lives, they have been known to amass a respectable competence and return to their own countries, to end their days in comparative respectability.

Such was the experience of a European woman, whose later history contains an element of comedy. She served for twelve or fifteen years in a certain brothel in Bombay, and by dint of steady thrift and much patronage she saved a considerable sum, which under advice she invested from time to time in local stocks and shares. At length, feeling that she had travelled far enough along the *via dolorosa*, and desirous of seeing her homeland once more, she decided to realize her stock and bid adieu to the East. Accordingly she called one morning at the office of the editor of a well-known Anglo-Indian newspaper, and enquired whether the editor, who granted her an interview, could advise her as to how she could best sell her shares. The editor, who questioned her about her history and plans, promised to introduce her to an English share-broker, who occupied an office in the same building; and when the latter happened a few minutes later to look in at the editor's office, he was informed of the lady's wishes. At his request, she drew from a large bag a bundle of shares and other papers, which he carefully looked through. Having done so, he told her that he could dispose of them for about Rs.10,000. 'Ah,' she replied in broken English, 'I thought my Consul was trying to cheat me; I took the shares to him first, and he offered me Rs. 3,000 for them.' The broker sold the stock; the lady received the due amount and departed by a foreign steamer to her own country, after expressing her gratitude to both the editor and the broker for their assistance. Two years passed, and the editor had almost forgotten the incident, when he suddenly received from abroad a letter and a small parcel. The letter was from the retired harlot, who recalled the matter of the sale of her shares to his memory, thanked him again for what he had done for her, informed him that she had married a man who was prepared to turn a blind eye to her past career, and that she had purchased a refreshment saloon in her native town with her savings, and finally begged his acceptance of the gift enclosed in the parcel. The gift proved to be a scarf-pin, of a preposterously unsuitable character, set with three large stones: one white, one red, and one blue. The editor kept it as a curiosity for some little time, studiously refraining from wearing it, and eventually, on receiving an invitation to the wedding of a friend, sent the pin as a gift to the happy bridegroom, without, of course, mentioning its origin. History does not relate what the bridegroom did with the pin; but it is certain that his wife would never have permitted him to wear so unsuitable an ornament.

The case of this woman was, however, exceptional. For, usually, these unfortunates become acquainted during the early years of their career with male procurers, panders and traffickers, who, before the War, made a practice of visiting at intervals the brothels in Egypt, India and the Far East, in which the women happened to be residing, and there took from them all the savings which they might have made in the course of their trade. Apart from this, European prostitutes are nearly always careless and unthrifty, and are frequently indebted to the mistress of the brothel for the cost of wearing apparel and other necessaries. It is, therefore, extremely difficult for a woman to shake herself free of the trammels of the trade. The male procurers, who belong largely to the Jewish faith and are mainly responsible for the preponderance of Jewesses in the brothels of the Indian coast cities, acted also, before the War, as information agents, advising women in Cairo, Alexandria and elsewhere of vacancies in the Indian and Far Eastern brothels, arranging with the brothel-keepers for their reception, if they desired to start in a new country, and often advancing the money for their steamer tickets, if they were short of funds. Being nearly always illiterate and generally uneducated, the women fall an easy prey to these unscrupulous agents and rarely escape from their indebtedness. With the object of enabling the police to deal more speedily and effectively with these peripatetic panders, the Indian Government has, since 1918, strengthened the provisions of certain enactments; so that, whether European prostitution eventually disappears from India or not, one may at least hope that the Jewish pimp from Eastern Europe and the Levant will find it advisable to exclude India from his despicable itinerary.

The brothels, in which these foreign European women reside, are invariably managed by a 'mistress', who is usually a 'time-expired' prostitute and is not supposed herself to practise her trade. This unwritten rule, however, is frequently broken, if the mistress is still fairly young and the inducement offered is sufficient. As a general rule, the mistress confines herself to the management of the house, and to acting as intermediary between the women and the male *clientèle* of the brothel; and in return for feeding and housing the women, she claims, and is paid, fifty per cent. of their earnings. The business has hitherto been fairly lucrative, as is proved by the sum paid for the goodwill, whenever brothels have changed hands. In the better houses the women are well treated, and are on the whole well looked after; and although they are not bound by law to do so, most of the houses employ a doctor, who inspects the inmates at regular intervals and certifies them free from disease. The houses are usually confined to a particular area and are sometimes distinguished by a red lamp hanging in the porch or verandah; a few poorer women live in single rooms, often opening directly on to the street, and live a more sordid and miserable life. The urban police keep themselves informed of new arrivals and of what takes place in the disreputable quarters, and are not slow to deport any woman, whether mistress or prostitute, who is guilty of misbehaviour. Although, as stated above, these European prostitutes come voluntarily to India, and are well over the age of 21 when they first arrive, it is probable that some of them may originally have been victims of the 'White Slave trafficker'; but so much time has elapsed since the original offence took place, and the women are almost always so very reluctant to bear witness against their betrayer, or 'fancy-man', as they style him in their jargon, that there is no chance of successfully prosecuting one of these international procurers in the Indian courts. Executive action alone is possible; and the amendment of certain Acts, to which reference has been made above, is likely to have a salutary effect in preventing foreign procurers from paying flying visits to India, as they have in the past, and therefore in diminishing indirectly the number of women of European nationality who visit India for the purpose of prostitution. A case did occur a few years ago, in which a woman of Creole descent from Mauritius was decoyed from her home to a Bombay brothel; but she had not been more than six or eight hours in the house before the police heard of her quandary and rescued her. She was handed over to the League of Mercy, a local vigilance society, which arranged for her repatriation to Mauritius, while the woman into whose clutches she had been inveigled by misrepresentation was arrested and deported from India.

Whether a reduction in the number of European professional prostitutes is likely to lead to an increase of vice among European and Eurasian girls domiciled in India, is a moot point. Much clandestine prostitution is known to exist among the latter class in large cities; and some people, with possibly a recollection of Lecky's famous passage of rhetoric, believe that if the professional prostitute were to disappear, her place would gradually be taken by those who are obliged by economic and other causes to sell their favours secretly. Even if this result did not follow, there might be increased resort to Indian women; and this possibility cannot, for several reasons, be regarded with equanimity by those responsible for the general welfare of India. Ceylon has in some quarters been held up to public approbation for having a few years ago expelled all the European prostitutes in Colombo. Closer investigation might possibly show that this drastic measure had provided a stimulus to other forms of vice of an equally deplorable character. Direct interference with prostitution in the spirit of the fanatical reformer has never proved wholly satisfactory in the past, and is on the whole of doubtful utility. It is wiser to work around the evil, circumscribing its orbit and taking stern measures against those who make a profit out of the trade. India is now a member of the League of Nations and has associated herself with the conventions and agreements arising out of the International Conferences on the Traffic in Women and Children; and she may therefore be trusted to follow the example of other countries in their crusade against 'commercialized vice.'

Before leaving the subject of prostitution, a word may be said about the offence of rape. There is no doubt that this offence is from time to time committed in Indian brothels, after young girls have been kidnapped, sold, 'adopted', or otherwise introduced into such places. But evidence sufficient to support a prosecution is often difficult to obtain, and the entire absence of public opinion among the social strata which would naturally become cognizant of such an offence, whenever committed, is mainly responsible for the paucity of prosecutions. Ordinary rape is not on the whole a very common offence, to judge by the annual returns: but it is probable that some cases are never reported to the police. In 1921 the total number of true cases of rape was: in Burma, 174; in the Panjab, 142; in the Central Provinces, 121; in the United Provinces, 65; in Madras, 31; in the North-West Frontier Province, 24; in Behar and Orissa, 36; and in Assam, 13. The number of cases occurring in any one of the large cities does not exceed ten a year, and is generally less.

CHAPTER V

MISCELLANEA

CRIMINAL TRIBES

IN the preceding chapters various references have been made to the activities of recognized criminal tribes, and there is little doubt that the future welfare of India and her claim to be regarded as a civilized country depend very largely upon her success in weaning these large bodies of nomads from their hereditary and traditional anti-social occupations. The problem is complicated by the fact that large numbers of such tribes belong to the territories of Indian rulers and potentates, where little or no attempt has hitherto been made to deal effectively with them. Rajputana, for example, shelters people like the Baurias, Sansis, Minas, Kanjars, Bagris, Bhils, Badaks, Bahelias, Aherias, Barias, Bhatus, Naths, etc., who subsist chiefly on crime, and regard the whole of British India as their happy hunting-ground. To these and other tribes of the same character, belonging to the provinces of British India, the larger cities offer an irresistible attraction. Calcutta has its Moghya Doms, Bhars, Palwan Dosadhs, Barwars, Pasis, Kewats, Tutia Musalmans, and many others, who serve to swell the crime-returns and constitute a constant menace to property; Bombay is visited by Chhoras and Baurias from Gujarat, by Mang Garudis, Phanse Pardhis and Kanjars from the Deccan, by Pathans and Waddars from Khandesh, by Uchlias, Bhamptas, Ramosis and Mangs from the Deccan, and by Wagris, Phadgadis, and many others; Madras likewise wages perpetual war against a large number of criminal tribes belonging to various districts of the presidency, among whom may be mentioned particularly the Kallars, the Chenchus, the Korawars and the Erukulas.

For those who wish to learn in detail of the lives, habits and customs of such tribes, there is no lack of material. Such works as that of M. Kennedy, on the criminal tribes of the Bombay Presidency; of Papa Rau Nayudu, on the criminal tribes of India and on professional poisoners and coiners of Major Gunthorpe, on the criminal tribes of Bombay, Berar and the Central Provinces; of Muhammad Abd Al-Ghani, on the tribes of the Madras Presidency; the volumes of the Ethnographical Survey of India; and various other standard publications—these give all the information at present available about the vagrant criminal tribes of India, and incidentally show how serious is the problem confronting the Indian Police. The latter endeavour to curtail the criminal activities of these tribes by constant resort to the Criminal Tribes Act; but the number liable to be 'registered' under that Act and to be placed under surveillance is so large that it often becomes impossible to watch them effectually. The constant movement of the gangs from province to province also leads to complications and to an overwhelming burden of correspondence, which hardly leaves the police officer any time for important duties nearer home. Behar and Orissa, for example, which has quite enough to do to control its own bad characters, suffered in 1920 from the depredations of Karwals, hailing from the Central Provinces and foreign (i.e. Native State) territory, and of a band of Nonias, described as an offshoot of the tribe of Chain Mallahs in the United Provinces. In 1921 the Kistna District of Madras was overrun by 'foreign' criminals, and consequently recorded more 'property stolen' than other districts. Other provinces and tracts tell the same tale. The country is so large, the criminal tribes so numerous, communications often so bad, facilities for escaping surveillance so many, and the police, as a whole, so inadequate numerically for the duties expected of them, that the effective control of these criminal nomads becomes practically impossible. Many members of criminal tribes are adepts at adopting a disguise, particularly that of *Gosavis*, or wandering mendicants and ascetics, which affords them easy access to inhabited areas. The Bhamptas of the Deccan are particularly fond of sending one or more of their number in this disguise into towns and villages, in order to spy out the land and secure information of likely premises to rob. There is no more effective disguise for an Indian than the dress of a Shaiva or Vaishnava ascetic, and many a criminal has owed his escape from arrest to his ability to play the rôle of one of the hundreds of wandering friars, who spend their lives in ceaseless peregrinations to the shrines lying between the Himalayas and Cape Comorin. Students of Maratha history will remember that it was in this disguise that the great Sivaji escaped from Aurangzeb's clutches at Agra; in recent times it has been adopted on occasions by members of the revolutionary party in Bengal.

While the police do their best to circumscribe the activities of the criminal tribes and keep their members under observation with the help of the provisions of the Criminal Tribes Act, various efforts have been made during recent years by official and non-official agency to wean some of these people from their vagrant and criminal life and accustom them to more settled and reputable means of livelihood. Chief among the non-official agencies is the Salvation Army, which has opened settlements in various places, notably in the United Provinces and in Behar and Orissa; while the Governments of Madras and Bombay have established somewhat similar settlements in various districts under their control. In the former province excellent work has been accomplished towards reclaiming the Kallars, a turbulent tribe of professional robbers and housebreakers; special schools and industries have been established for them, which in consequence of the devoted labours of an able and sympathetic Indian official have met with a large measure of success. The same can be said of some of the settlements in the Bombay Presidency, including Sind, where the troublesome Hur tribe is now under control. Attempts are now being made to settle other criminal tribes of Sind, such as the Jagiranis, Khushks, Jokhias and Kirias, who have long been a source of trouble to the public and the police. In the presidency proper, the Deccan and the Carnatic, or Southern Maratha country, are the home of a large proportion of the wild tribes of western India, and it is for them that settlements have been established in Sholapur, Hotgi, Barsi, and other places in the southern districts.

There are seven settlements or more in the United Provinces, which contain a considerable number of criminal and degraded tribes. Of recent years, also, some tribes have made certain spontaneous efforts towards self-reform, by sending their children to village schools and so forth. Unfortunately, these efforts, which deserve every encouragement, have been rendered fruitless by the hostile attitude of the upper classes of Indian society. Schoolmasters, who doubtless reflect the views of their pupils' parents, have resented and actively discouraged the entrance to their schools of the children of criminal tribes. Two boys of this class, who were sent by a local official to the Government school of carpentry for training, were so grievously persecuted that they were forced to leave. 'Such hatred and opposition', runs the official report, 'on the part of the higher castes are met with everywhere, and have proved an almost insuperable obstacle to the moral and social improvement of the criminal tribes.' This denunciation is not overdrawn; the paralysing fetters of caste hold the whole of India in bondage; and the men who talk most glibly about equal rights for all races in Kenya Colony never raise a protest against the unsympathetic and frequently inhuman treatment, accorded by the Indian upper classes to the lower, or untouchable, tribes and castes. When one finds a provincial legislature solemnly refusing permission to certain low-caste Indians to draw water from a well or reservoir used by persons higher in the social scale, when one reads of the children of nomad tribes denied entrance to primary schools, one listens with some impatience to the vociferous claims of the Indian politician to be granted equal rights with the pioneers of other nationalities in foreign and undeveloped lands. As remarked above, Provincial Governments in India have made definite efforts to reclaim some of the more troublesome and turbulent criminal tribes; but the ultimate civilization of these human survivals of past centuries of rapine and disorder can never take place, until India shows a change of heart and her upper classes realize, which they do not at present, that they have a duty towards their degraded and unfortunate compatriots.

In some cases the task of reclaiming these tribes is almost insuperable. A pamphlet, issued by the

Madras Publicity Bureau in 1921, records a protracted struggle on the part of a young police officer to reclaim the wild Chenchus of the Nalamalai hills. The pamphlet describes them as a forest tribe living in small villages in Kurnul, and earning their living partly by collecting forest produce, by grazing cattle, and by hunting. No small share of their livelihood is derived from theft, dacoity and the levy of blackmail from the neighbouring peasants and from the pilgrims who visit the Srisailam temple. All observers agree in describing them as idle, improvident, drunken, thievish and brutal. They are not remarkable for intelligence, but they have learnt to distil arrack and to manufacture serviceable bows and arrows; some of them are in possession of fire-arms. At home, they burn the forest in order to pick up more easily the *ippa* flower, which they distil. They then get drunk, quarrel and shoot one another. They are expert bowmen; and no constable, forest watcher, or excise peon dares to interfere with a Chenchu carrying his bow and arrows. A pilgrim or peasant who tries to protect his property from the Chenchus has a poor chance of life.

By 1914 the Chenchus had become so serious a nuisance that the Madras Government appointed a special officer to get into touch with them and try and induce them to give up dacoity and burning the forests. For two years he worked among them, teaching them to cultivate the land. He worked with his own hands side by side with the Chenchus in the field, hoping by his example to overcome their idleness. He grew mulberry bushes and obtained silk-worms from Mysore. The lac insect was introduced from the Central Provinces. He arranged with the Forest Department to provide the Chenchus with regular cooly work; he opened schools for them, and when the trained teachers fled in terror, he recruited the best substitutes he could find in the neighbouring villages. He enticed the Chenchu children to the school by a bait of parched rice and *dholl*; he tried to teach them physical drill, the habit of washing, and the game of football. The obstacles in his path were serious. The trained school teachers were frightened away by fever and arrows; the moment the children felt bored, they vanished into the jungle, and school hours had to be curtailed; cholera, small-pox and drought made their appearance. The indolence and intemperance of the Chenchus defeated all efforts to establish village industries among them; and the police officer's own health began to give way under repeated attacks of malaria.

At the same time Chenchu crime commenced to increase rapidly, partly in consequence of the protection which the Chenchus had recently received from the attentions of the ordinary police. For, to give the special officer every chance of winning the confidence of the Chenchus, the district police had avoided all interference with their villages. Consequently the Chenchu bad characters enjoyed unusual immunity in their marauding enterprises, and were able to demonstrate to the rising generation that it was possible with a minimum of risk to gain by one night's crime far more than could be earned by six months' honest labour. This school of thought naturally acquired a considerable vogue, and the special officer found it impossible to counteract its effects. At last, therefore, after two years' devoted work and much fever, the special officer had to own that his labours 'did not seem to be leading anywhere'. The experiment had been a failure, the kind of failure that is no less honourable than success. The Chenchus could not be reformed until they had been taught the primary lesson that crime does not pay. To open schools and offer co-operation to the Chenchus in their present temper was, in the words of the District Magistrate, 'like offering chicken bones to a tiger'.

Difficulties of the Police

Many are the obstacles to the successful prevention and detection of crime that confront the Indian police officer. In Burma, where serious crime is said to be increasing, the chief factors militating against successful work are reported to be (*a*) unintelligent investigation, (*b*) want of public spirit, (*c*) imperfect presentation of cases in court, (*d*) the cleverness of many criminals, (*e*) the law's delays, (*f*) the practice of tampering with witnesses, (*g*) want of courage on the part of the public in resisting malefactors, (*h*) fear of reprisals, (*i*) the unsuitability in a primitive country of the western system of criminal procedure and the law of evidence, and the scepticism of the courts. While some of these factors are operative in other provinces, the two chief obstacles confronting the police in India proper are probably public apathy and magisterial delays. As regards the former, every province makes the same complaint, namely, that the police receive little or no assistance from the general body of citizens, while of recent years their apathy has been in many places exchanged for an attitude of uncompromising hostility. In the Panjab, for example, more then fifty per cent. of the crime committed is professional, i.e. burglary and cognate offences; yet the public has not yet grasped the fact that co-operation with the police, in order to secure the punishment and control of the criminal, is really self-help. In the

United Provinces, as in other parts, the employment against persons of evil repute and bad livelihood of the useful preventive sections of the Code of Criminal Procedure is often prevented by the impossibility of getting respectable persons to give evidence against them. This reluctance to bear testimony to facts within their knowledge is usually ascribed to the fear of reprisals, and also generally to a rooted distaste of being involved, even as a witness, in a police prosecution. Of late years, also, a certain sympathy with the doctrine of 'non-co-operation' has increased the general disinclination to assist the police in their primary task of preventing crime. 'The laws in force in India', wrote the Inspector-General of Police, Bombay Presidency, in 1920, 'have been based on the English model, on the somewhat erroneous assumption that "the man in the street" is actively on the side of law and order against the criminal. In the past, one of the most formidable obstacles to successful police work in India has been the apathy of the public and the absence of public spirit as it exists in England. To this obstacle has now to be added non-co-operation, in its acute or sub-conscious form, which throws the police more than ever on their own resources. In the circumstances the wonder is not that the number of undetected cases is so high, but that it is not higher. The explanation lies in the fact that detective ability is inherent in a large number of the Indians serving in the police.' This expression of opinion is equally applicable to other provinces. The police are friends to none, and by many are actively disliked and opposed. They have to carry out their heavy task of preventing and detecting crime under difficulties which the police of western countries can hardly conceive.

Delays in the hearing and disposal of cases by the courts are common throughout India, particularly in rural tracts; and even in the large cities, where magistrates are permanently stationed and sit regularly in court from day to day, inordinate delays sometimes occur. Mr. Justice Rowlatt's Committee drew pointed attention to this evil in their report on anarchist conspiracies in India. They quoted, among other instances, a trial for murder, which commenced at Alipore on January 2nd, 1917, and had not been decided in April, 1918. Though no witnesses had been called for the defence, the trial had lasted 63 days, and the counsel for one of the accused had addressed the court for 20 days! The crime, it may be added, had taken place in August, 1916. A notable instance occurred in Bombay in 1910, where an ordinary case of rioting, which should not have occupied more than six days, absorbed 35 hearings and lasted for five months. Much of this delay was due to the policy of procrastination adopted by the pleaders engaged in the case, who are often adept at finding excuses for postponement and adjournment. In the districts these delays are disastrous from the police standpoint, for they serve to impair the witnesses' memory of events and thus weaken their testimony, and they also give the defence ample chance to win over the witnesses for the prosecution. The case of murder in Burma, quoted in an earlier chapter, exemplifies the latter point. Moreover, in rural tracts the magisterial court is generally situated, or held, at some distance from the witnesses' homes; and the latter, who often have to make a lengthy journey, only to find at the end of it that the case is postponed on one pretext or another, become greatly discouraged, and endeavour as best they can to wash their hands of the case. There is little doubt also, as has been mentioned under the head of theft, that many persons are dissuaded, by the fact of this dilatory magisterial procedure, from seeking redress through the police and the courts. These delays, however, are not invariably due to the practice of adjournment for flimsy or inadequate reasons. They are almost inseparable from a system under which the magistrate in the district, *taluka*, or *tahsil*, has a variety of executive and administrative duties to perform. In Behar and Orissa, for example, where the hearing of a case *de die in diem* is practically unknown, constant remands in 1921 were chiefly due to the magistrates being engaged in revenue, census, electoral, famine, flood, and miscellaneous duties, and also to the transfer or death of magistrates, whose total number is usually insufficient to cope with the volume of case-work. The same is the case in other parts of India, notably in Assam, which reported that transfers of magistrates in 1921 resulted in constant *de novo* hearings of partly-heard prosecutions, while additional delay was caused by the wilful non-attendance of parties and witnesses, and by the difficulty of tracing the antecedents and proving the previous convictions of old offenders.

To these obstacles to the successful prosecution and conviction of offenders has been added in recent years the open antagonism engendered by the doctrine of non-co-operation. In normal years it is hopeless to expect any improvement in the percentage of undetected cases, unless the police can count upon assistance from the Indian public, and—it may be added—the Indian Press. Since certain well-known firebrands were permitted to sow the seeds of disorder broadcast through India, open refusal on the part of the public to give the police any help, or even to allow others to do so, has been the order of the day; and although, in consequence of the incarceration of the leading agitators, outbreaks of grave disorder have become less frequent, it will take several years of dead-lift effort to restore conditions in which the police can feel sure of even a modicum of co-operation. The ordeal through which the Madras Police passed in 1921 has been quoted in an earlier paragraph. Their experiences have been shared by their comrades in other provinces, who, besides being hampered in the performance of their ordinary duty, have on several occasions faced serious injury and death at the hands of misguided mobs. While the European police officer, in city or district, is expected as a matter of course to make head against a sea of troubles and keep ugly situations well in hand, it is little short of surprising that the Indian rank and file have borne themselves with such remarkable courage and fidelity during the almost intolerable strain of the last few years. It is against the police that the secret wire-pullers and the seditious newspapers have poured forth their bitterest venom, and it is the police who, with very little encouragement from the Indian Government and none from the new Legislative Councils, have made a stand against those who sought the overthrow of the administration.

The difficulty of ordinary police work, particularly in respect of detection of crime, is aggravated by the inferior character of the village police, upon whom they are supposed to depend specially for information of events in outlying tracts. In the Bombay Presidency the police *patel* is far from satisfactory; in Bengal the *chaukidar* is generally regarded as useless. The latter is very poorly paid—in Behar and Orissa he is supposed to receive from Rs. 2-8 to Rs. 5 per month—and his pay is usually in arrears. In Assam, where the *chaukidars* in some districts are described as more helpful, their pay is never received regularly on the due date, and some *chaukidars* actually appear to prefer the reiterated promises of the village *panchayats* to hard cash. Such being the sole agency upon which a numerically inadequate force has to depend for information of crime committed, or likely to be committed, over a vast tract of country, it is not surprising that many offences remain undetected or that many offenders escape punishment. The police are not so much to blame for this result as the system, which obliges them to depend upon a poorly and irregularly paid collection of village agents, who are survivals of a vanished age.

The pay of the police themselves is inadequate, and has not been everywhere increased to correspond with the general rise in the cost of living and the multiplication of the duties now assigned to them. 'The Sub-Inspector', so runs a recent official report, 'is the pivot round which the force revolves. An efficient sub-inspector generally means an efficient police station. Upon his shoulders lie heavy responsibilities, and he is met at every turn by temptations to dishonesty. Yet the sub-inspector, when he emerges from the probationary stage, is given a salary which barely suffices to secure a good cook in Bombay or an indifferent chauffeur. From him the public expects education, breeding, intelligence, initiative, integrity and loyal service. All these attributes the public should have, but they must be prepared to pay for such qualities in their servants.' In most provinces the constable is no better off in the matter of remuneration than his superior officer. Even before the days of the Montagu-Chelmsford reforms, the

Government was chary of setting aside large sums of money in the budget for the purpose of augmenting the pay of the rank and file, and in one notable instance they were only compelled to do so by a constables' strike. Nevertheless, concessions in the matter of pay have been made during the past ten years, though even with these the constable in many areas is still underpaid by comparison with the wages earned in industrial and private employment, and often finds it a matter of great difficulty to support himself and his family. Proposals for an increase of pay to the police have never been viewed very sympathetically in the past; it is unlikely that the new legislatures, which now control the provincial expenditure, will show any keener desire to remove the grievances of this large and heavily-worked body of public servants.

Bad housing is another disability which exercises a pernicious effect upon police efficiency. This is particularly noticeable in the large cities, where, in the absence of official lines or barracks, the men are forced to live in insanitary tenement-buildings, which are productive of fevers and other ailments. Bad housing, indeed, has a closer connexion with the prevalence of crime and the paucity of detected cases than is generally imagined. This was clearly shown in Colombo, where in 1917 the most criminal quarter of the town possessed no accommodation for a police station or for the police attached to it. The men were thus forced to find rooms wherever they could in hired hovels, and were in hourly association with the criminal elements. The consequent loss of self-respect, lack of discipline, etc., were reflected in a heavy crime sheet and a corresponding lack of detection. Within two years of proper buildings being provided, crime was more than halved and detection more than doubled. Housing conditions in Bombay City were deplorable, until the Local Government decided, a few years ago, to impose upon the City Improvement Trust the task of providing police stations and housing accommodation in various parts of the town and island. Older members of the force can remember the day when one rather important section possessed no police station; the officers of the section registered complaints in the verandah of their residential quarters; inquiries were conducted in the dressing-room of a fourth-rate native theatre; while the sectional records and constables' kit-boxes and the station dead stock were housed in an odoriferous native tea-shop. Conditions in Bombay are now far better; but though many of the constables are at present well housed, their barracks are built in insanitary localities; and this, coupled with the strain of continuous point-duty in a thoroughly enervating climate, saps their vitality and results in an unduly large percentage of admissions to hospital. At the present day the Bombay Police are, on the whole, more suitably and adequately housed than their *confréres* in some other provinces. In Bengal new buildings are very badly needed, and in Behar and Orissa the force is reported to be disgracefully housed and inadequately clothed. Suitable dwelling accommodation and suitable official buildings are indeed the primary need of the Indian police in all provinces, and so long as present conditions exist, the Government can hardly expect any great change for the better in their general health and efficiency.

Lastly, the performance of miscellaneous duties, which have no direct connexion with the prevention and detection of crime, reacts unfavourably upon police work throughout the country. Chief among such duties, which absorb much time and distract the attention of the police from their regular activities, may be reckoned the serving of notices and processes for the courts. Two instances will suffice. In 1917 the Bengal Police served 204,000 processes. In 1921 the Panjab Police served 284,000 processes, which naturally involved an enormous waste of time and the neglect of far more important work. The experience of other provinces is the same; and in the cities, also, constables have constantly to be released from point or beat duty for the same purpose.

Such are some of the disabilities which clog the activities of the police in India. There is, perhaps, no other country in the world, claiming to be civilized, in which more is expected of the police and less is given to them in the way of encouragement and material advantages. The Government periodically hands out a string of decorations and indigenous titles, or issues an official eulogy of the work of the police; but the rank and file in some provinces still find themselves handicapped in the struggle for existence by inadequate emoluments and wretched housing. They meet with no encouragement from the general public, whom they are appointed to protect from violence or loss, or from the legislative bodies, which are supposed to sanction the funds necessary for their proper maintenance and general efficiency. In the circumstances it is remarkable that the police should have come through the ordeal of the last few years with so much credit and success. The following extract from the *Report upon the Moral and Material Progress and Condition of India*, for the year 1918-19, gives a succinct and faithful view of the duties and disabilities of the Indian Police:—

> 'Some idea of the difficulties to be encountered can be gathered from a consideration of the diverse

work, which the force responsible for peace and order may be called upon to perform at the same moment. At one place in India, the police may be cautioning a taxi-cab driver for exceeding the speed limit; at another place they may be fighting pitched battles with mediæval brigands; at a third they may be tracking down anarchists of a malevolence and fanaticism equal to anything that even Bolshevist Russia can boast. Year in and year out, under multifarious conditions, the ceaseless battle between the forces of order and disorder goes on. Upon the issue of the struggle, India's prosperity to-day and her progress in the future very largely depend. In this struggle, the brunt of the battle is borne by the police. To them more than to any other body of servants is due the peace which is the first essential of all progress. Yet, despite their services, the police are not popular in India. The Indian-edited Press can as a rule see little good in what they do: if they interfere to prevent a meeting, which they think may lead to a breach of the peace, they are accused of attacking the most precious liberties of British subjects; if they come into conflict with a mob and disperse it efficiently, they are attacked for using violence against harmless citizens. If, through excess of caution, they fail to nip rioting in the bud, they are blamed for inefficiency and indifference. If, working under conditions of exceptional difficulty, they fail to check anarchical crime, their failure is at once commented upon in bitter terms; on the other hand, should they carry precautionary measures to the extent of arresting persons against whom no case can be proved to the satisfaction of the public, they are denounced even more fiercely. In short, for all their work, the police are little trusted by the vocal section of Indian opinion. . . . In India the constable is not looked upon as a friend of the peaceful citizen, so much as his potential oppressor. Partly, no doubt, this regrettable attitude is a heritage from bad old days, which India still too clearly remembers, when executive authority was synonymous with arbitrary power. Partly, it is due to the actual existence of a limited amount of petty oppression on the part of ill-paid subordinates, which, despite the best efforts of the upper ranks, is not yet completely eradicated, although becoming rarer day by day. Principally, however, it may be surmised that this attitude arises from the fact that the police, being the arm of the administration which comes most frequently into contact with the people at large, becomes unconsciously identified with the administration itself in the minds of all those who are discontented with the existing régime. As a consequence, the police have to some extent to carry upon their shoulders a burden of criticism which should properly be shared among all departments of Government.'

GAMBLING

Gambling has been known in India from days of remote antiquity. The *Arthasastra* of Kautilya proves that under the Mauryan Empire it was looked upon as a vice and was strictly prohibited in military camps; but recognition of its evil effects did not prevent the Mauryan Government from appointing a Superintendent of Gambling, whose duty it was to concentrate the practice in one or more central licensed premises, and recover for the State five per cent. of the winnings of each player, as well as fees for the hire of dice and other apparatus and for the supply of water, etc., to the gamblers. The inveterate addiction of the Rajput tribes to gambling has been described by Tod (*Annals*), who compared it with the gambling propensities of the German tribes, described by Tacitus. At the present day, gambling is carried on in the capital cities of most provinces, assumes various forms, and is unquestionably responsible for a certain amount of crime. In 1920, the Calcutta Police prosecuted 668 cases of gambling in the courts; and from time to time the police of Bombay and Madras and other centres carry out raids upon important gaming-dens. The districts outside the presidency towns are not by any means free from the gambling craze; but except in Burma, where petty gambling is fairly ubiquitous, it is not so much in evidence as in the large urban centres. In 1921, the Burma Police recorded nearly 4,000 prosecutions for gambling, and in the opinion of the local authorities the number ought to be even larger, in view of the very real connexion between gambling and crime in that province. Any reluctance on the part of the police to deal with petty forms of gambling results automatically in a general increase of the gambling craze and a corresponding increase in the number of thefts; while several of the districts can quote concrete cases, in which gambling was the direct cause of serious crime, including murder and robbery.

Bombay has always been notorious for gambling, whether in the form of the well-known *teji-mundi* contracts, the *ank-satta* or opium-gambling, or ordinary gambling with dice and cards. Up to 1890 the extraordinary form of wagering known as rain-gambling was also prevalent in that city. It used to take place during the monsoon at a certain open space, where a house was rented at a high price for the four months of the monsoon by a group of Indian capitalists. In one form of rain-gambling, wagers were laid as to whether the rain would percolate in a fixed time through a specially-prepared box filled with sand, the bankers settling the rates and odds according to the appearance and direction of the clouds. In an alternative form, winnings or loss depended on whether the rainfall during a fixed period of time was sufficient to fill the gutter of a roof and overflow. The wagering usually took place between 6 a.m. and 12 noon, and again between 6 p.m. and midnight, and was held responsible for so much loss that the authorities put a stop to it by legislative and executive action.

A form of bagatelle, styled *eki-beki*, was likewise abolished by police action during the last decade of the nineteenth century. But ordinary gambling with dice and cards flourishes, in spite of police action, and is as much a feature of the lower life of the bazar as is the wild speculation and gambling in 'futures', which distinguishes some parts of the business quarters. At intervals the police pay special attention to the vice and secure a temporary improvement; but as soon as vigilance is relaxed, the evil reappears and rapidly increases.

The promoters of gambling are usually adept in the art of misleading the authorities. They rarely use the same room on successive occasions; they have elaborated a vocabulary of warning-calls; and they employ spies and watchmen to keep them posted in the movements of the police. It seems probable that the subordinate police occasionally accept hush-money to turn a blind eye on the gamblers' movements; for otherwise it is difficult to understand why men, who are known to have been running gambling reunions for years, should have successfully evaded the law, and in one or two cases have accumulated a considerable fortune in the process. The task of the police in checking gambling is not rendered easier by the fact that at certain Hindu festivals social custom and tradition sanction gambling as an integral feature of the celebrations; and although the custom at such seasons may be less evident than it used to be thirty or forty years ago, it is still possible for the police on such occasions to arrest quite a number of respectable Hindu merchants and charge them with an offence under the Gambling Act. The illegal gambling, as distinguished from speculation that does not traverse the law, which is carried on in 'futures', opium, silver, etc., is responsible for a good many cases of criminal breach of trust and misappropriation, particularly among the clerks, agents and servants employed by the big Hindu business houses; while the gaming with dice and cards, in which deliberate cheating is not unknown, is the indirect cause of much petty crime against property. The punishment inflicted upon persons convicted of offences under the Gambling Act is nearly always a fine of varying magnitude, which has little or no deterrent effect. Nothing short of a term of imprisonment is likely to wean the hardened organizer of gambling parties from a form of livelihood, which brings him considerable profits without much risk.

The tendency of gambling to incite to crime is illustrated by an extreme case which occurred in Bombay in 1915. A body of Pathan gamblers, who had a dispute about the cards and the wagers, tried to settle their differences by a free fight, in the course of which one of the gamblers, Muhammad Khan, fired a revolver several times and injured some of the opposite party. The police arrested the whole gang except Muhammad Khan (who contrived to escape for the time being), and secured their conviction for rioting and causing grievous hurt. Some months afterwards, the Criminal Investigation Department received information that Muhammad Khan had returned to Bombay and was running a gambling-house. The information was passed on to the divisional police, who raided the house and arrested sixteen gamblers, among them being Muhammad Khan. He was put on his trial for attempted murder, rioting, and causing grievous hurt, and was convicted and sentenced to seven years' rigorous imprisonment.

Cocaine

The habit of cocaine-eating is a growth of the last twenty years or so, and before the outbreak of war in 1914 it had obtained an extraordinary hold upon the lower classes in the cities and larger towns of India. An opinion was current a few years ago that resort to cocaine-eating was partly due to the embargo placed upon the wholesale consumption of opium, and that inability to procure their regular supplies of the latter drug drove the masses to the far more pernicious use of cocaine. Whether there be any foundation of truth in this view or not, the fact remains that by the year 1909 the vice had attained very large proportions, and even women and children had fallen victims to a habit, which plainly exercised a most deleterious effect upon their health and morals. Little notice was taken, by the authorities, of the prevalence of the habit, until 1903, when the High Court of Bombay decided for the first time that cocaine was a drug included within the definition of 'intoxicating drug' in the Bombay Abkari (Excise) Act. Since that date the illegal sale of cocaine in India has greatly expanded, and every Provincial Excise Report bears testimony to the spread of the 'cocaine habit'. 'The consumers of the drug, which is notoriously harmful, are found in all classes of society; but in India, as in European countries, the drug is mostly used by prostitutes, or by men as an aphrodisiac. The habit has spread chiefly to those classes which are forbidden by religion or the rules of caste from partaking of liquor and the well-known Indian intoxicating drugs.'

The bulk of the supplies of the drug, smuggled into India, come from Germany, and bear the mark of the well-known firm of E. Merck of Darmstadt. This firm issues cocaine in flat packets of various sizes, ranging from one to three ounces, which are easily packed away with other articles and greatly favour the methods of smugglers. The smuggling and distribution are so cleverly organized that it is extremely difficult to trace and prosecute the persons who really control the import and distribution of the drug. One individual, in fact, who before the War was strongly suspected of international dealing in cocaine, was known never to touch a single grain of the drug himself, or to keep any in his possession. The first real check to the traffic, which is international in character, was provided by the drastic restrictions on imports and exports imposed after the declaration of War in 1914, and by the sudden cessation of the Continental steamship companies' traffic between Europe and the East. But even this respite was not of long duration; the profits to be made out of the traffic are too tempting to be lightly relinquished by the dealers; and no sooner had imports from Germany and Austria been definitely suspended than imports of the drug from Japan commenced to find their way into India, and became an almost equal danger. Most of the Japanese cocaine hitherto seized bears the mark 'Sanscido and Co., Kobe', and it is usually imported by Chinese and Japanese sailors, of whom the former often exchange the cocaine for Indian opium, which is smuggled into China on the return journey.

Sailors, stewards, firemen, and sometimes engineers and officers of foreign vessels, are the chief smugglers of cocaine from Europe, which is introduced through the ports of Bombay, Karachi, Calcutta, Madras, Marmagao, and Pondicherry, and great ingenuity is employed in passing the drug through the customs houses at those places. The supplies, when they escape detection, find their way to certain inland distributing centres, namely, Delhi, Lucknow, Meerut, Lahore, Multan, Surat and Ahmedabad; and of these places Delhi is especially notorious. The retail trade in the towns is likewise characterized by great cunning, and those involved in the traffic maintain a regular army of watchmen and patrols, whose duty it is to shadow the excise and police officials and give the alarm when a raid is contemplated. One of their most daring coups was the seduction, in 1913, of the private chauffeur of the Collector of Customs at Bombay, whose motor-car and servant would, they knew, be regarded as above suspicion. He used to take charge of smuggled supplies and transport them in his master's car to his own quarters and when he was eventually caught by a joint raid on the part of the police and excise officials, much cocaine was found in his possession. The case exemplifies the saying that the darkest place is immediately under the lamp.

The police and excise officials, who wage perpetual war against the smuggler and retail trader, have from time to time secured very large hauls of the drug. In 1911, an Austrian steward was arrested with 300 grains concealed in the soles of his boots; in 1912, an English police officer secured the arrest of a fireman from a German vessel with 40 lbs. of cocaine, valued at Rs. 46,000, in his possession; in 1913, two Muhammadan police officers traced a large consignment, valued at Rs. 17,000, to a house in Bombay City; and two Indian constables discovered 4,500 grains in the possession of a Hindu merchant. In 1914, three constables, engaged on an inquiry into a case of crime, found a wooden box locked up in the room of a woman of the washerman (Dhobi) caste. The woman gave the name and address of the owner of the box, which was found to contain 1,700 grains of cocaine; and a further search resulted in the discovery of nearly 54,000 grains. A saloon waiter, who was found in possession of 50 grains as he was leaving the Bombay docks, confessed that he had purchased the supply from a Muhammadan, who imported it into Calcutta from Rangoon; and two head constables, who stopped a fireman of a P. and O. vessel on suspicion, found 8,000 grains tied round his thighs. It must be admitted, however, that such arrests and seizures, which occur continually, do not secure any real diminution of the traffic from abroad. They do upset the local market for the drug and interfere temporarily with the supply of the tiny paper packets, which are sold by agents in the more disreputable streets. But even when the vigilance of the authorities has checked supplies for the moment, the retail dealer, nothing daunted, has palmed off powdered magnesia and Epsom salts on the unfortunate victims, who are naturally unable to complain of the deception. In the ordinary way, too, the drug is often adulterated with quinine and phenacetin, in order to enhance the enormous profits of the retail trade. It is estimated that the price per ounce of cocaine purchased from the wholesale dealers varies from Rs. 100 to Rs. 120, and when sold by the grain the retailer realizes from Rs. 400 to Rs. 425 per ounce.

Local seizures of the drug and prosecution of offenders have so far failed to put an appreciable check upon this illicit traffic; and considering the enormous profits involved, this is hardly a matter for surprise. The Bombay Police prosecuted 31 persons for illegal possession of the drug in 1921; the United Provinces reported in the same year that cocaine smuggling was on the increase; and many prosecutions for illegal sale and possession took place in other centres. Burma alone reports that, owing to prohibitive prices, the demand for the drug is said to be diminishing; yet seven districts of that province reported captures of cocaine in 1921, the largest quantity seized in a single haul being 24,000 grains. Moreover, in Rangoon up to that year it was the policy of the authorities to regard opium and cocaine dens in one particular section of the town with a certain amount of toleration, on the ground that these dens were the resort of criminals, and thus in a sense facilitated the surveillance of bad characters. But this policy was very properly abandoned in 1921, and the cocaine dens were closed down. Morally there was no justification for their existence, for the cocaine habit has ruined many young Burman boys; and even school-children in Burma are said to have fallen victims to the vice. Moreover, while indulgence in opium cannot be said to lead directly to crime and many opium smokers are not prevented by the habit from performing their daily work, cocaine invariably leads to petty crime, such as pocket-picking and street-thieving, and rapidly reduces its victims to a condition in which they cannot do a stroke of honest work. A cocaine maniac is always distinguishable by the condition of his tongue, upon which the drug, when eaten, appears to have a marked effect; and the casual visitor to a police station in the more disreputable sections of an Indian maritime city will often see the inspector-in-charge call upon a prisoner, who has been brought in under arrest, to put out his tongue. A moment's glance is sufficient. 'You are a cocaine-eater?' remarks the Inspector; 'Yes', replies the prisoner; and there is a general consensus of opinion among the staff of the station that on that account the charge against the prisoner, probably of theft or brawling, is likely to be true. The cocaine-eater, if he belongs to the lower strata of Indian society, as is usually the case, is nearly always addicted to crime. He cannot apply himself to any task; the craving for the drug is invincible; and he therefore seizes any means, however illegitimate, to procure the money required to pay for a regular supply of it.

Legislation and strict preventive measures appear to be powerless to put an end to this illicit traffic, which is really international in character. Since the conclusion of the War, the whole question has been the subject of discussion at Geneva under the auspices of the League of Nations, and the opinion seems now to be generally accepted that the evil can only be adequately countered by stringent supervision of the primary sources of supply and joint action on the part of all the States concerned. The sooner some international scheme of this kind can be devised, the better will it be for the moral and physical welfare of those unfortunates in the West, as well as the East, who cannot withstand the lure of a harmful and insidious poison.

Opium

Crooke (*Things Indian*), commenting upon the fact that opium is not mentioned in Sanskrit literature or in the works of the earlier Muhammadan historians, suggests that its cultivation probably spread from Europe, where one variety of poppy was grown by the Swiss lake-dwellers. Sir George Watt considers it probable that 'the merits of the poppy seeds and poppy capsules were known to the Arabs and to the people of large tracts of Central Asia, and even of upper India, anterior to the supposed Greek discovery of opium. But the silence of the early Sanskrit authors leaves no room for doubt that right down to the commencement of Muhammadan influence in India the various wild poppies of the country attracted very little attention.' Barbosa, the traveller (1511-16), is the first European writer to describe Indian opium; Garcia da Orta, the Portuguese physician (1574), speaks of Cambay opium coming from Malwa; while in the time of Tavernier the Dutch used to export the drug from Burhanpur. Crooke, who collected these references, was inclined to believe that, as tobacco-smoking came into use in the sixteenth century, the smoking of opium began in imitation of it, at a time long subsequent to the establishment of the habit in China. Under the Mughal emperors the drinking of opium was a common mode of assassination. A decoction was made by crushing poppy-heads and allowing them to soak in water for a night. 'This', wrote Bernier, 'is the potion generally given to princes confined in the fortress of Gwalior, whose heads the monarch is deterred by prudential reasons from taking off. A large cup of the beverage is brought to them early in the morning, and they are not given anything to drink till it be swallowed.' Tod and Malcolm describe the *kusumbha*-drinking in Rajput *durbars*. 'The minister used to wash his hands in a vessel placed before the Raja, after which some liquid opium was poured into the palm of his right hand. The first in rank present approached and drank the liquid. The minister again washed his hands, and served a dose to the second in rank, and so on. To appease a feud, they used to drink opium from each other's hands, an almost sacred pledge of friendship. Tod adds that, to judge by the wry faces on these occasions, no one could like it, and to get rid of the nauseous taste comfit-balls were served round. Even at the present day the Rajput of Cutch and Rajputana drinks a cup of opium-water, after he has smoked and bathed on rising, and this he shares with any friends present.'

The use of opium has attracted considerable attention from critics outside India, while in the country itself the consumption of opium and hemp derivatives excites little reprobation, provided that the use of these drugs is not carried to immoderate lengths. Indeed, the whole position of opium differs entirely in India and in western countries, and a correct appreciation of the peculiar features of the opium question in India is not secured, but rather is hindered, by the piles of literature emanating from well-meaning but ignorant philanthropists in other countries. The Indian Government rightly complains that most of these ardent reforming spirits have no first-hand experience of the Indian position, and that in consequence of the fact that it is directly connected, for administrative convenience, with the opium trade, it has been subjected to wild and unmerited accusation. According to the *Report upon the Moral and Material Progress of India in 1921*, the Government of India has been accused in some quarters of corrupting souls and ruining bodies for its own selfish purposes, in India, China, and elsewhere.

According to the official statement just mentioned, the broad facts of the opium question are as follows: The soil of most parts of India will produce the opium poppy. The population of India habituated itself, for many centures before the arrival of the British, to the consumption of opium in small quantities. The vast majority of the people connect this drug, and to some extent justifiably, with certain medical properties. At the height of the early plague epidemics in the closing years of the last century, the keeper of an opium club in an Indian city boasted that of his regular customers not a single one fell a victim to the disease, despite the fact that people were dying all round them. The people also use opium on ceremonial occasions, and they cannot and will not be broken of the habit suddenly. The total consumption per head is very small; for opium is not widely smoked in India, but is employed rather as a household remedy and as a refreshment on ceremonial occasions. As in the case of drink, the policy of the Government of India is to control the trade in such a way as to ensure its most effective regulation, and to prevent it from passing into the hands of the type of person, with which it would readily, if uncontrolled, become associated.

For more than a century, Government has been engaged in the gradual acquisition of control over the production, transit and sale of the drug through the continent. This has been done by the practical concentration of the cultivation, so far as British India is concerned, within restricted areas; by the discontinuance of cultivation in many of the Indian States as the outcome of negotiations; and by the inclusion of the different provinces in the general system, as the necessity for regulation becomes manifest. The success of this policy is proved by the fact that, while the revenue from opium steadily rises, production and consumption steadily decline decade by decade. Rising prices and restricted supply are gradually causing it to be used less and less for ceremonial hospitality or personal indulgence, and are tending to restrict its consumption to purposes more strictly medicinal. A typical example of this process is found in the figures for the Madras Presidency. In 1911-12 the consumption of opium was 41 thousand *sers*, producing to the State a revenue of £0·13 million. In 1920-21, the consumption had declined to 36 thousand *sers*, while the revenue had risen to £0·23 million.

Offences under the Opium Act are not uncommon, and occasionally large seizures of illicit opium are made. In Mandalay, for example, in 1921 nearly 21,000 *tolas* of opium were seized by the police and the excise authorities, one of the most notable offenders being a European dentist, who was found to have 9,000 *tolas* concealed in his luggage. Opium from the Southern Shan States is often smuggled into Thayetmo, and a case occurred in 1921 in which a Shan smuggler, when challenged by the police, who suspected him of being an absconder, attacked the arresting officer with a *dah* and had to be shot. He was said to have concealed a very large amount of opium, before he was killed by the police.

In carrying out their opium policy, the Government of India are rather handicapped by the existence of the

Indian States, which cannot be subjected to the rules and regulations applicable to British India. As a result of negotiation, some of the States have adopted the Government policy in regard to the production of opium; but, while no opium produced within their territory can pass into British India without a permit, the Government of India can exercise no effective control over their production of opium for internal consumption. 'To attempt to enforce any policy of suppressing or restricting the cultivation of opium in Indian States, apart from any arrangements which may be entered into under treaty obligations, would mean an interference with their internal administration such as the Government of India have no power to exercise, either by prescriptive or by treaty rights.' So far as the consumption of opium in India is concerned, the Government asserts that its policy has met with definite success.

The habitual opium-eater, who is occasionally to be found in the cities, indulges usually in what is termed *madak* or *chandu*, which is prepared by boiling down the rags in which the grower collects the essential juice of the product, and inspissating the infusion. The use of the drug in this form is undoubtedly demoralizing, and the consumers of it generally belong to the degraded classes (Crooke, *Things Indian*). The 'clubs' in the large cities, in which opium-smoking is carried on, are as a rule squalid places in the more odoriferous parts of the bazar. The shutters are tightly closed, the walls, once whitewashed, are grimed with dirt and smoke, and occasionally are ornamented with chromo plans of famous places of pilgrimage, representations of Hindu gods, or perhaps oleograph portraits of British Royalty. The smokers lie all over the floor in groups of four or five, each of them being provided with a little wooden headrest, and lying curled up like a tired dog, with his face turned towards a feeble oil lantern in the centre of the group. Each smoker holds an opium-pipe, consisting usually of a bamboo stem and a small china bowl of the ink-pot type, and into the latter he inserts at intervals a tiny pellet of opium, which he first heats in the flame of the lamp at the end of a long needle. The room is heavy with vapour and very airless, for every chink and cranny in the shutters is covered with fragments of old sacking to shut out the night air. The smokers belong to various classes and types. A Sikh embroiderer from the Panjab may be resting alongside a Muhammadan mechanic from the railway workshops; a Native Christian clerk beside a Hindu refreshment-room keeper; or a pedlar beside a member of the seafaring class. In one such 'club' the author of this book once discovered a Muhammadan girl, dressed in the coat and knickers of a Goanese or Native Christian boy. Her parents had died when she was only two or three years old, and having no relatives to whom she could be sent, she had been adopted, so to speak, by the habitués of the opium den, who gave her sufficient food to keep her alive in return for her services as a menial and messenger. The girl was apparently not quite in her right mind, and on this account, perhaps, raised no objection to donning the boy's garments provided for her by her patrons. The object of the smokers in cutting her hair short and dressing her in male attire may have been to disarm inconvenient enquiry, and possibly to protect her against rape. She appeared to be perfectly satisfied with her surroundings, which could not well have been more squalid or better calculated to foster disease, and replied to all questions regarding herself with a vacant but attractive smile.

Occasionally the frequenters of these opium dens amuse themselves by playing a game peculiar to this phase of night-life. Two men squat on the floor, in face of one another, with their backs against the wall. Each of them holds between his knees a long-stemmed pipe, terminating in a fair-sized metal bowl, which rests on the ground. Into these bowls they push from time to time a small round ball of lighted opium, mixed with some other substance, and then, after a long intake of breath, they blow down the long stem with all the force of their lungs, so that the lighted pellet leaps from the bowl in the direction of the adversary. The game is to make seven points by hitting one's opponent so many times within a fixed period, and the score is counted by the players' adherents or backers, of whom each player generally has two or three squatting beside him, who gamble in a mild fashion on the result. The winner of the contest receives the exiguous stakes for which they play. The game cannot be described as brisk, for both players and onlookers are generally in a more or less comatose state; but the interest which they take in an occasional hit is obviously genuine, and keeps them from succumbing entirely to the lethargic atmosphere of the place.

The *kusumbha* dens of an Indian city are on the whole a little less dirty and odoriferous than the rooms in which opium-smoking is carried on; but, like the latter, they are visited by a motley assortment of people of various castes and classes. The following description of a *kusumbha* den was published a few years ago by an Englishman who had investigated the habits and customs of a large Indian urban population:—

'At length on the second storey a half-open door casts an arrow of light upon your path. You hail it with joy after the gloom of the lower floors, and, pushing the door open, you find yourself in a square, low room, lit by two windows, which command a view of the street below. It is carpeted with cheap date-leaf mats and a faded polychrome *dhurri*; dirty white cushions are propped against the wall below the windows; a few square desk-like boxes stand in front of the cushions; and in a semi-recumbent attitude round the room are some twenty or thirty men—Bombay and Gujarat Muhammadans, men from Hindustan and one or two Bohras, who are the regular customers of the *kusumbha* saloon. There is one woman in the room, a member of the frail sisterhood, now turned faithful, nursing an elderly and peevish Lothario with a cup of sago-milk gruel, which opium-eaters consider such a delicacy. The other customers sit in groups, talking with the preternatural solemnity born of their favourite drug, and now and again passing a remark to the cheery-looking landlord with the white skull-cap and henna-tinged beard.

'Each occupant of the room has been provided with a tiny glass of weak opium-water from the large china jar on the landlord's desk, and pays one pice per glass for the beverage. Some drink one glass, some two, some three or more; but, as a rule, the *kusumba* drinker confines himself to two glasses, being ashamed to own even to a brother *Tiryaki* the actual quantity of the drug consumed by him. A few, strengthened by prolonged habit, pay something more than the usual price for a thicker and stronger dilution. When the glasses are empty, the company calls for dessert, for the opium-drinker must always have his *kharbanjan*, or bitter-taste-remover, and the landlord thereupon produces sweets, fruit, parched gram, or sago-gruel, called *khir*, according to the taste of his customers. Hardly has dessert ended, when an elderly Muhammadan in shabby dress falls out of the group and, clearing his throat to attract attention, commences to recite a flowery prelude in verse. He is the *dastan-shah*, own brother professionally of the *sammar*, or story-teller of Arabia, and the *shayir* of Persia and Egypt; and his stories, which he delivers in quaint sing-song fashion, richly interspersed with quotations from the Persian poets, are usually culled from the immortal *Thousand and One Nights*, or are concerned with the exploits and adventures of one of the great heroes of Islam. Amir Hamza, for example, is a favourite subject of the imaginative Eastern story-teller. Amir Hamza, according to Professor Dryasdust, died before the Prophet, but according to the troubadours of Islam was the hero of a thousand stirring deeds by flood and field, and by the might of his right hand converted to the faith the Devs and Peris of Mount Kaf (the Caucasus). You will hear, if you so wish, of his resourceful and trusty squire, Umar Ayar, owner of the magic *zambil* or satchel, which could contain everything, and master of a rude wit, similar to that of Sancho Panza, which serves as an agreeable contrast to the somewhat ponderous chivalry of the knight-errant of Islam.

'Thus the *dastan-shah* helps the time to pass until 8 p.m., when the club breaks up, and the faded Aspasia helps her fractious Pericles down the rotten staircase and out into the night. Ere the company departs, each member subscribes a pice for the story-teller, who earns in this way about forty pice a day—no inconsiderable income in truth for the mere retail of second-hand fables. Then with a word of peace to the landlord the men troop slowly forth to their homes'. (*Byways of Bombay*, 1912.)

On the whole, the consumption of opium presents few of the evil results associated with the use of alcohol in Europe, and it does not incite men to crime in the same way that intemperance and the cocaine-habit do. Most of the regular smokers of opium are not prevented by the practice from performing their day's work, and it is possible that, as many smokers assert, the daily consumption of the drug has a certain prophylactic value against disease. The only form of crime which can in some cases be traced directly to the habit is petty pilfering by penniless persons of the beggar type, who lack means to purchase their daily supply of the drug. It is certainly less dangerous to the individual than the constant or excessive use of the products of the hemp-plant, *ganja*, *bhang*, and *charas*.

Drink

The use of intoxicating liquor has been known in India from time immemorial, and the prevalence of drinking in ancient days is attested by the directions in the Code of Manu, that members of the higher castes who indulged in spirits were to commit suicide by drinking them in a boiling state, and by the action of a reforming potentate of Cape Comorin, who used to brand wine-bibbers with a hot iron. The rise of the impure worship of the *Sakti* or Mother-goddess, expounded in the *Tantras*, which was celebrated by the use of animal food and spirituous liquors, indulged in to excess, and terminated with promiscuous carnal copulation on the part of the initiated, undoubtedly was one of the main causes of the spread of drunkenness among the lower classes. (See Crooke, *Things Indian*, for further references.) It is wholly absurd to suppose, as some misguided people have done, that liquor-drinking is a product of British rule in India, or that the immoderate use of spirits has increased during the last two centuries. Streynsham Master referred in 1672 to the abundance of drink consumed by the people of Surat; Buchanan-Hamilton, speaking of Bengal in the early years of the nineteenth century, wrote: 'In no country have I seen so many drunken people walking abroad; and in more than one instance I saw men, who, from their dress, were far above the vulgar, lying on the road perfectly stupefied with drink, and that in the middle of the day, and in places far removed from the luxury and dissipation of towns.' Lastly, Colebrooke remarked of Nagpur in 1800:—

> 'The number of distillers' shops is incredible. Mahrattas of all ranks drink immoderately, and so do the women. Even ladies of rank use spirituous liquors; but the women who fetch wood and grass from the forests, are, most of all, addicted to intoxication. It is curious to see of an evening crowds of well-dressed women getting drunk at a distiller's door.'

Such scenes as these are unheard-of at the present day, and the drink problem, as understood in western countries, is practically unknown in India, save in the few places where heavy concentrations of industrial workers occur in congested conditions. 'Throughout the countryside and in the smaller towns, while there is too much drinking to please the social reformer, the figures of average consumption are extremely moderate as compared with those of any other country in the world.' So runs the official *apologia* of 1921, which adds that 'the policy of Government in the matter of drink and drugs is to bring the traffic under strict control and to derive the maximum revenue from the minimum consumption. Temptation to those who do not drink is minimized, and excess is discouraged among those who do. Government heavily penalizes illicit manufacture and consumption, and endeavours to restrict the habitual consumer to liquor shops, instead of allowing him to employ illicit sources. The control which Government thus obtains over the drink traffic enables hours to be shortened, houses to be reduced in number, liquor to be reduced in strength, and temperance propaganda to be carried on effectively. The Indian liquor shop bears not the least resemblance to the inn or saloon of western countries. It is situated as a rule on the outskirts of the town; it is extremely unattractive both in inward and outward appearance; and is calculated to serve the need merely of those who are habitual consumers. Moreover, Indian liquor shops are comparatively few and far between. In the Central Provinces, for example, which stands roughly midway between the extremes of excise revenue per head of the population, there is only one liquor shop for every 3,415 persons and for every 24 square miles.'

Nevertheless, there is a good deal of illicit distillation and consumption in India, which is facilitated by the ease with which access is obtained to illicit sources of supply. 'In south India, and for the matter of that in many districts of northern India, liquor can be had from almost any palm tree, with no more skill than is required to cut an incision and with no more apparatus than a knife and a toddy-pot. In a country where so large a proportion of the lower or labouring classes are accustomed to the use of liquor, and where every man can, so to speak, have his beer tap in his own back garden, the mere closure of shops can have little effect in stopping recourse to alcohol.' Cases of illicit distillation and consumption are by no means easy to detect; and the Commissioner of a large division in the Central Provinces, in drawing attention to the figures of crime against the excise law in 1921, averred that comparatively few cases of illicit distillation are detected. He added the warning that if the policy accepted by the Government of working towards complete prohibition is to be followed to its natural conclusion, it will be necessary not only to make large additions to the preventive excise staff, but also to increase the police, in order to deal with the disturbances which are bound to ensue on the greater activity of the preventive agency.

In the large cities of India there is a great deal of drinking to excess, particularly among the industrial population, who live in crowded and insanitary tenement-buildings and are very prone to drown their difficulties, discomforts, and disease in the liquor shop. A certain amount of urban crime can be attributed directly to drink, as, for example, in Rangoon, where there were 664 prosecutions for drunkenness in 1921 and thirty-one of the total number of important crimes were the direct outcome of intemperance. These crimes included murder, culpable homicide, grievous and simple hurt, assault, theft and obscene behaviour in public places. In Bombay City, where in one official year 4½ million people consumed about 1¾ times as much country spirit as the 11½ million people in the rest of the Presidency, drunken brawls and other offences are fairly frequent, particularly on the occasion of Hindu festivals, like the *Holi*, which is traditionally characterised by much licence in every direction. Europeans in India are acquainted with the type of servant who asks his master for definite permission to get drunk; and, as Crooke remarks, the servant can generally state the precise amount which will produce the desired effect. There is also a good deal of drinking among lower-class prostitutes in the cities and their degraded supporters and *clientèle*, and intemperance is often the predisposing cause of the disturbances and complaints of theft or assault, etc., which emanate from those squalid areas. In one case the cinematograph and drink were jointly responsible for the forcible abduction of a girl. Four men, of whom one was enamoured of a young woman belonging to a different community, entered into a conspiracy to kidnap her by the methods shown in a sensational film, which was being exhibited in one of the native theatres. They accordingly primed themselves with drink, hired a motor car, and, having by a ruse secured her, drove her out of the city by night at a break-neck pace. The speed was too hot to last, and the car came to grief about twelve miles outside the city. The culprits were eventually arrested, and the girl restored to her relatives.

Though the evil effects of drink are more noticeable in the cities than in rural tracts, the Government is *per contra* in a position to take more drastic steps to meet the evil in urban areas. They can arbitrarily reduce consumption by limiting the amount of liquor to be issued; they can reduce the strength of the liquor issued; they can limit the hours of consumption; and they can forbid shops to sell liquor except for consumption on the premises. In these various directions Government intervention is now being tested; while both in the cities and elsewhere much solid work for temperance is being carried out by missionary societies, the Y.M.C.A., and indigenous philanthropic bodies. The genuine progress, to which these bodies direct their efforts, must be sharply differentiated from the deplorable temperance crusade, engineered and prosecuted during recent years by the followers of the misguided Mr. Gandhi. 'Throughout India', in the words of the *Report upon Moral and Material Progress for 1921*, 'the non-co-operators and other rash adherents of the temperance movement managed to interfere seriously with the business of the liquor sellers. Pickets were placed around shops, and drinkers subjected to various forms of insult and degradation. They were excommunicated from their caste, deprived of the services of barbers and washermen, beaten, garlanded with shoes, tied to poles, or driven through the streets on the backs of donkeys with their faces to the tails. The tangible effect of this misguided energy was to excite popular reprobation, not against the habit of drinking, but against the habit of buying drink from Government shops. In certain cases, incredible as it may seem, ignorant persons were informed that, after the ruin of British power had been accomplished, they would be in a position to brew their own drink without hindrance. Hence, during the period under review, while the Government revenue fell off seriously in certain parts of India, there is little reason to believe that the total consumption of liquor by the population diminished to any considerable extent. From certain provinces, indeed, it is reported that illicit drinking has grown to a height unknown of recent years.'

The latter result was apparent both in the Central Provinces and Burma in 1921. The Inspector-General of Police in the Central Provinces reported that the temperance campaign led to a great deal of unlicensed distilling in Mandla, and that, the number of cases being greater than the excise staff could deal with, orders had to be issued to the police to take up cases *suo motu.*

Incidentally this led to an increase in the number of prosecutions under the Arms Act; for, in their search for illicit stills, the excise officers often discovered unlicensed arms. The Superintendent of Police, Mandalay, wrote as follows in the same year: 'I am informed that the political agitation in Burma, among both Burmans and Indians, with its semi-social crusade against drinking, gambling and other vices, has given a fillip to the illicit liquor trade. Our noble patriots find that they cannot go openly to liquor shops, as they were wont to do, because of the bad example they would set, and so, though they continue to preach against drink and the vicious Government, which encourages liquor shops for the sake of the revenue it brings in, they themselves have recourse to illicit manufactures for the supply of the cup that cheers and, thank Heaven, also inebriates.' Whether the formation of temperance societies will be successful among Burmans is a moot point, but it seems clear that such a movement finds no sympathy among the Indian coolies working in Burma. The Superintendent of Police, Pegu, recorded in 1921 a definite attempt by agitators to enforce temperance among the Indians in that district, with the usual accompaniment of violence and intimidation. The attempt was quite fruitless: the Indian cooly insisted upon having his liquor. So will it be in India. The Government under pressure from the indigenous politician may, if it wills, abolish all liquor shops and destroy its distilleries; but the Indian labourer and worker will still demand his drink and will obtain it. And so long as the lower classes can obtain a supply of liquor, the police will have to deal with a certain amount of crime directly traceable to intoxication and the excitement caused by excessive consumption. In the words of Gibbon, 'the wines of Shiraz have always prevailed over the law of the Prophet.' Even so, the toddy and mhowra liquor of India will always set at naught the injunctions of the Indian legislature.

Anonymous Communications

The habit of anonymous letter-writing is well-known in India. There are few Government officials who have not at one time or another received such communications, purporting to inform the recipient of alleged malpractices or misbehaviour on the part of his Indian subordinates, and the character of even the higher European officials is sometimes impugned by means of anonymous letters addressed to the Provincial Government. The waste paper basket is usually the final resting-place of these slanderous messages. Letters of this type are often addressed to private individuals, with the object of intimidating them or making them feel uncomfortable; and it must be added that some Indians of standing allow themselves to pay more attention to these cowardly communications than they are worth. Threatening letters were received by several Government officers during the progress of the anarchist conspiracies of a few years ago, and in some instances they led to very necessary precautions being taken against injury and assassination. Occasionally, in the case of criminal inquiries by the police, anonymous letters have proved valuable, by giving clues to the perpetrators of offences or to the whereabouts of stolen property. A case in point was the murder of a wealthy young Bhattia widow in Bombay, to which reference has been made in an earlier chapter. The police were working wholly in the dark until a day or two after the discovery of the crime, when the Commissioner received an anonymous letter in Hindi, which resulted in the speedy arrest of the murderers. It subsequently transpired that the letter had been written by one of the gang, who considered that he had not received a fair share of the property looted from the murdered woman's house. Similar communications have led to the discovery of other crimes, and to the tracing of arms and ammunition in unlawful possession.

As a rule, it is practically impossible to trace the authorship of anonymous letters, and except in the case of communications having reference to current police inquiries, it is generally the merest waste of time to attempt the discovery of the writer. A case, however, which occurred in Bombay in 1915, and was eventually unravelled by the police, contained such curious features that it seems worth while to record the details. For more than two years the Criminal Investigation Department was engaged in an attempt to trace the source of several series of objectionable and highly-defamatory anonymous postcards and letters, which had been received from time to time by high officials, prominent public men, and clubs. Any event of public interest—political, social, or personal—resulted in a shower of typed postcards, addressed to officials or their wives, and to persons connected directly or remotely with the event. The postcards were usually defamatory, scurrilous, and sometimes flagrantly indecent, and were sent not only to Bombay residents, but also to officials in all parts of India, to the Viceroy and even to H.M. the King. The C.I.D., after close scrutiny of a number of the cards, were able to establish the fact that all of them had been typed on a single machine. They were also able to identify the class and make of the machine; but they were unable to carry their inquiry further, until they arranged with the authorities of the General Post Office to allow them to scrutinize all postcards received in the post office during a fixed period. The method adopted was as follows: a head constable, who was conversant with all the details of the type in question, sat for a period of fourteen days or more in the large general letter-box, and picked up and scrutinized every postcard as it was dropped into the box from outside.

His patience was at length rewarded. One day a postcard fell through, which presented the same features and faults of typing as appeared in the anonymous cards. A closer examination proved beyond doubt that it had been typed on the machine for which the police were searching; and as the card in this instance was a *bona fide* business communication, the police were able at once to locate the machine and continue their inquiry. The machine proved to be the property of a well-to-Indian resident, and, as it appeared unquestionable that he himself was the author of the cards, he was duly arrested, charged with an offence under Section 292 of the Indian Penal Code, and released on bail. While the police were engaged in collecting further evidence to support the charge, the accused, who had many influential friends, confessed to one of them that he was the author of the anonymous postcards, and asked his advice as to what course to pursue. His friend advised him to make a clean breast of his guilt to the Commissioner of Police, and beg for mercy.

The accused agreed to his friend's advice, but eventually thought better of it. A day or two later he managed to burn himself so severely, while ostensibly lighting a gas stove with the help of a bottle of methylated spirit, that he died in a few hours. The circumstances of the case caused some commotion in a section of the community to which the accused belonged, and the usual attempts were made to explain away or to hush up the matter. The police, in particular, were urged to refrain at the inquest on the accused from making any allusion to the criminal inquiry which was in progress at the time of his death. But as several wild rumours in relation to the case had gained currency in the city, some of which were designed to place the police in a false or equivocal position, the latter decided to make no reservations, and to reveal the facts in so far as they were relevant to the sudden death of the accused. There is no doubt that the accused committed suicide, in order to avoid the stigma of a prosecution and probable conviction; but the coroner's jury played up manfully to the wishes of the deceased's friends, and returned a verdict of accidental death. The plague of anonymous postcards ceased abruptly on the arrest of the accused.

FINGER-PRINTS

The system of identifying criminals by means of their finger-prints and keeping a record of impressions was first elaborated and adapted to Indian conditions by Sir Edward Henry, formerly Inspector-General of Police in Bengal and afterwards Chief Commissioner of the Metropolitan Police. The system is now well-established in India, and most provinces maintain a central finger-print bureau as a branch of the Criminal Investigation Department. The number of finger-print slips on record gives some idea of the large number of criminals dealt with by the police. In 1921, the total number of slips in the Madras bureau was 228,000 in round figures; in the Punjab, 300,000; in the United Provinces, 211,000; in Burma, 135,000; in Behar and Orissa,

135,000; in Bombay 115,000; in the Central Provinces, 80,000; and in Assam, 25,000. The Calcutta, Bombay, Madras and Rangoon police also maintain their own bureaux. The number of slips annually received for enquiry by the provincial bureaux varies from 1,200 in Assam to 19,000 in Bombay and 32,000 in the Panjab, and the number of prisoners and accused persons identified annually by the bureaux totals to about 6,000 in Burma and the Punjab, 4,000 in Madras, and 3,000 in Bombay. The Bombay City Bureau, which has about 70,000 slips on record, received 7,500 slips for search in 1921, and out of this number identified 1,830 criminals.

Instances of the utility of this system of criminal identification are constantly occurring. For example, a dacoity with murder occurred in 1921 in the Akola District of the Central Provinces. A gang of Pardhis were arrested on suspicion; but the evidence was considered insufficient for conviction, except in the case of one man, whose finger-prints were discovered on some torn papers left near the scene of the dacoity, after their removal from the complainant's house. In another case a man was arrested for swindling at Cuttack, who on inquiry was proved to be a notorious inter-provincial swindler, wanted under another name by the United Provinces Police. He absconded while on bail, leaving behind him his mistress, Rukmini Bai. She was found by the bureau to be identical with Radha Bai, who was jointly concerned with her paramour in the swindling case in the United Provinces. Bombay City provided an interesting example in 1916. A case of house-breaking and theft occurred, in which the police had no clue to work upon, until a constable noticed that the thief, who had evidently lighted a lamp to facilitate his crime, had left a faint finger impression upon the chimney of the lamp. This mark was treated so as to render it opaque, and it was then photographed and enlarged. This photo-print was compared with the finger-prints of a man suspected of being concerned in the case, and was found to be identical with that of the right index finger of the suspect, a criminal with five previous convictions. With this evidence to help them, the police were able to secure the conviction of the house-breaker and recover a fair amount of the stolen property. In another instance finger impressions enabled the police to trace and arrest a Muhammadan, who had fraudulently obtained a telegraphic money-order from Bengal, which rightly belonged to a pilgrim on his way to Mecca.

The police of the larger cities also find the bureaux of great use in identifying deportees, who have returned in contravention of the original order of deportation. This occasionally happens in the case of criminals belonging either to foreign countries or the territories of Indian princes, such, for example, as the Marwadi from Jodhpur, who systematically defrauded Indian prostitutes to such an extent that the women appealed to the police for protection. A more gruesome, but very necessary, task that falls on these bureaux is the identification of the corpses of unknown persons. In 1921 the Panjab bureau received 271 slips relating to unidentified corpses, and in 26 instances it was necessary to dissect the skin from the fingers of the deceased and prepare impressions from them. The bureau was able to identify twelve of the bodies as those of ex-convicts. The deceased in some instances had been murdered, and the revelation of their identity by the finger-print staff formed an important link in the police investigation. The bureau maintained at the headquarters of the Bombay City Police has accepted the additional task of recording the finger-impressions of all candidates for employment as sweepers in the Municipal Health Department. A series of thefts, carried out a few years ago by sweepers, whose duties afford them easy access to dwelling-houses, showed that several of the men employed were ex-convicts; and at the request of the municipal authorities, the police agreed to scrutinize the finger-impressions of all applicants, and to trace their identity in cases where they might have previous convictions. Two or three hundred persons are thus dealt with annually, out of whom a few have been proved from time to time to be ex-convicts passing under assumed names. The experts of these Indian bureaux are also frequently summoned to give evidence regarding finger-prints on documents, etc., in the civil as well as the criminal courts. An ingenious Bengali police officer compiled a few years ago a 'telegraphic code for finger impressions', which is said to be of considerable use to the police of outlying districts.

CHAPTER VI

CRIME AND INDIAN ASPIRATIONS

A PERUSAL of the preceding pages may leave on the mind of the reader an impression that India harbours an unduly large criminal population. But it must be remembered that a country which 'contains immense tracts of desolate mountain and jungle, which exhibits every gradation of cold and heat, luxuriance and sterility, loveliness and desolation, and which shelters one-fifth of the human race', cannot rightly be judged by the standards applicable to England or any civilized European country. Moreover, if it be true that the salient features of modern history are the development of nationalities and the growth of individual freedom, then India can hardly be described as essentially part of the modern world. 'It is a great continent in which there are no nationalities. The population is an immense mixed multitude in different stages of material and moral growth, exhibiting an extraordinary variety of peoples, creeds and manners. Much of India may still be regarded as the best surviving specimen of the ancient world on a large scale.'

During the last few years one has heard general statements made by ardent political evangelists regarding the great change which has taken place in India, and the immense strides made by the people towards national self-consciousness and the goal of political independence. This may be true of a minority of educated Indians, resident for the most part in the capital cities and larger towns; and efforts have been made to satisfy their awakened susceptibilities and political needs by constitutional experiments of a novel character. But the vast majority of the Indian people, whether ploughing the soil of the Deccan uplands, hoeing tea in Assam, cutting rice in the swamps of Eastern Bengal, doing scavenger's work in the streets of the provincial capitals, or earning a precarious livelihood as hunters and fishermen, have remained practically unchanged during the last hundred years or more, and save when they are directly incited by mendacious propaganda to rebellion and tumult, care nothing about politics, the State, or popular representation. 'What concerns them,' as a well-known official document puts it, 'is mainly the rainfall or the irrigation supply from wells or canals; the price of grain or cloth, the payment of rent to the landlord or revenue to the State, the repayment of advances to the village bankers, the observance of religious festivals, the marriage of their daughters, their health and that of their cattle. They are not concerned with district boards or municipal boards; many of them know of no executive power above the district officer, and of Parliament or even of the Legislative Councils they have never heard. In one province it is stated that 93 per cent. of the people live and die in the place where they were born.'

It follows naturally that much of the crime committed in India, as well as the difficulties encountered by the Indian police in their daily duty of preventing and detecting it, results from the inability of the mass of a caste-ridden people to comprehend the meaning of the terms 'State' and 'Society,' and therefore their own position and duty towards the latter. Crime in its widest signification has been said to consist of acts that are forbidden by law, and Law forbids those acts that are inimical to the cohesion of society. For such acts would, if permitted, result in the disintegration of society. The majority of the lower castes and classes of India, to say nothing of the various wild tribes of hereditary criminals, have not yet grasped these ideas, for they are still wholly illiterate, are influenced largely by animistic superstition, and possess very primitive habits and customs. They have not yet learnt, for example, that every citizen is bound by his duty to the State, not merely to abstain from hindering, but actively to assist in securing the arrest of an offender, and that he has a further obligation to justice to give true evidence at the trial of offenders, not to destroy or falsify material evidence, nor to induce others to err in either way. Hence it comes that responsible police officials in India constantly complain that they receive no help from the Indian public in detecting crime and arresting offenders; on this account much of the evidence produced in criminal inquiries is untrustworthy or deliberately misleading; on this account also maliciously false complaints and false suits are a fairly common feature of everyday life; and for the same reason attempts to influence police, magisterial, and sometimes also judicial, officers are not unknown.

So far as concerns such offences against the State as counterfeiting coin, forgery and the fabrication of false documents, and the personation of public servants, India is perhaps no more culpable than some European countries. The criminal records of Europe would give plenty of information about counterfeiters far more expert than the wandering Bauria and Chhaparband, who belong to primitive groups of aboriginal forest-dwellers that have never been given a chance to rise to higher levels; and forgery, likewise, is not an unknown charge in the English law courts. But in England certainly, and so far as is known in other European countries also, there is nothing equivalent to the false complaint, manufactured evidence, and destruction of evidence, such as many magisterial and police officials become acquainted with during their career in India. Nor are the authorities in England faced with a deliberate and wide-spread disinclination or refusal on the part of the public to assist them in bringing offenders to book. In England, if a murder is committed, every citizen regards it as his duty to assist the police in tracing and capturing the murderer. The Press is equally active, publishing all the information it can obtain regarding the circumstances of the crime and the description, etc., of the supposed offender. In India, on the other hand, the police have to carry out their duty unaided. The public, even if it does not go to the length of destroying or suppressing evidence and clues, gives no active support; while the average vernacular newspaper, with a few praiseworthy exceptions, is far too full of political criticism of the Government or advertisements of aphrodisiacs and quack remedies to find room for other matters.

It must not be supposed for a moment that the ordinary Indian peasant or industrial worker approves of the excesses of the criminal or is anxious to play the part of *particeps criminis*. On the contrary, he is by nature disposed to obey the behests of superior authority and objects generally to crimes of violence. But he has not yet assimilated the doctrine of the duty of the individual towards the State and society, and has been nurtured on the ancient tradition that the task of seizing and punishing offenders belongs primarily to the ruler as distinct from the subject. Coupled with his primitive estimate of the value of human life and his general ignorance, is a traditional and hereditary suspicion of the *bona fides* and methods of the police. No one who acquaints himself with the provisions of the *Arthasastra*, embodying the most ancient Hindu ideas of efficient administration, can deny that this traditional suspicion was once justified, and that the police of ancient days, and of later centuries also, frequently committed gross acts of oppression and tyranny. History indeed records instances of the populace being goaded to such a pitch of anger by such acts that they rose and assassinated the *kotwal* or other obnoxious official; and folk-tales still survive to attest the profound distrust of the police felt by the people of past centuries. The fact that in British India corruption and tyranny have now been greatly reduced in volume and character by determined action on the part of Government and its European officers, and that the methods of investigation now in vogue bear no resemblance to those which were common under Hindu and Moslem despotisms, ought to have resulted by this time in a keener public appreciation of the activities of the police and a stronger inclination to assist them in a very difficult task.

It is unfortunate that the educated Indian agitator, who has made continuous attempts of late years to rouse the temper of the masses, has not hesitated to malign and vilify the police wholesale, and thereby has not only counteracted any change for the better in the attitude of the public, but has also aggravated the traditional antipathy towards the guardians of law and order. It must at the same time be admitted that the apathy or hostility of the public, which unfortunately militate against the success of the district police in most provinces, are by no means so noticeable in the larger cities, which shelter numbers of the educated classes of Indian society. Bombay, for example, has recorded several instances in which private persons have assisted the urban police, even at the risk occasionally of serious personal injury, and on special occasions, which demanded extra police precautions, numbers of educated Indians have offered to enrol themselves as special constables and co-operate with the uniformed force. The police authorities of other cities have probably had somewhat similar experiences. There is little doubt that if education was as advanced in the villages as it is in the cities of India, the task of the police would be much lighter, and the labouring classes would be far less prone to being swayed by avowed extremists and revolutionaries, who urge them to disregard, if not openly to attack, the constabulary.

The primitive state of society throughout the greater part of the Indian continent is well known to students of Indian customs and religion, and is apparent in the frequency of such crimes as dacoity and highway poisoning, and in the extent to which the law of vengeance prevails. A backward glance into the history of the English race brings us very soon to a time when the vendetta was in vogue, when wrong-doing was punished by wrong-doing, when the relations of man with man, of family with family, and of tribe with tribe, were determined very largely by the motive of vengeance. The province of the criminal law, as has been said, is to supersede this system of private warfare by a method more impersonal and more just, and to leave it to a third party to mete out the punishment that is due to aggression. And the measure of the degree to which the spirit of legality has overcome the spirit of vindictiveness is a measure of the height of civilization of the community. Instances have been given in the preceding chapters which will suffice to justify the statement that the system of private warfare, or the blood-feud, or the spirit of vindictive retaliation, as the case may be, still form the basis of much of the crime committed in India, and further, that if by any chance the maintenance of the system of law and order imposed by the British upon India were to terminate, a large portion of the country would revert in an incredibly short time to the primitive code which prescribes an eye for an eye and a tooth for a tooth. The general chaos resulting therefrom would be aggravated, without a shadow of doubt, by the disintegrating influence of religious differences and religious intolerance. For the criminal tribesman, for the murderer, the dacoit and the robber, it would be the return of the golden age; and they would exact a full toll of vengeance from a society, which so far has denied them a share in the educational and other advantages enjoyed by the upper castes and classes. The lower ranks of the Muhammadan community, with their intense hatred of the idolator and *Kafir*, would lose no time in attacking, looting and murdering their Hindu opponents, and not a single educated Hindu or Moslem politician would be capable of restoring order or preventing atrocities, compared with which the anti-cow-killing riots at Arrah in 1917, or the sectarian riots at Agra in 1920, would be the merest child's quarrel.

The British politician of a certain type, be he Pacifist, Fabian, Socialist or Hebrew idealist, is too prone to judge India by the standard of the educated Indian fair-weather visitor to this country, who, in his desire to transfer to the hands of his own class the powers hitherto wielded by the British Government in India and its carefully-selected officials, slurs over or conceals the exceedingly primitive mentality and habits of three-quarters of the population of his country. Consequently, our philanthropists in and outside Parliament generally overlook the salient fact that human life in many parts of India is considered of very little account, and that the market-price of murder in even the more settled tracts is still very reasonable. Barely a century has passed since the Pindaris, composed of Indians of all provinces and all religions, were perpetrating almost incredible cruelties throughout India, ravishing and murdering women and children under the eyes of their husbands and parents, and leaving many villages wellnigh permanently desolate. The spirit of lust and avarice, which prompted those raids, still lives beneath the surface of Indian society, and has only been prevented during the last fifty years from again bursting forth in a maelstrom of destruction by a strong central government and a well-organized police force, led by European officers. There are, indeed, few countries in the world in which organized crime could develop so quickly as in India, where most provinces contain large tribes of professional and hereditary criminals and freebooters, large masses of illiterate peasants living on the margin of poverty, and an upper stratum of well-to-do people, among whose virtues and good qualities physical courage is not always strikingly conspicuous.

It will not be denied, presumably, that the primary internal function of the State is to keep the peace within its own borders, and its most important duty to substitute the ordinary arbitrament of law for the disorderly arbitrament of private war, in the settlement of disputes between its citizens. Hence it is of primary importance to suppress offences against the peace, whether they assume the menacing form of armed rebellion, as recently happened in Malabar, or whether they take the less important shape of riot or unlawful assembly, or are mere affrays between individuals. If this postulate be accepted, it follows that any proposal for complete self-government in India at this moment must be held premature and difficult to justify. For the educated classes of India, into whose custody the administration of the country would naturally be transferred, are not yet powerful enough in any respect to impose their will for peace and order upon the huge population of their rude and primitive compatriots. It is no exaggeration to say that, assuming the disappearance of English administrators and English executive officers from India, which is repeatedly demanded by the more extreme Indian politicians and finds an echo in the new Legislative Councils, crime, in the wide sense mentioned in an earlier paragraph, would cease to be under control, and would rapidly give rise to conditions fundamentally inimical to the Utopian dream of Indian nationhood and Indian *Svaraj*. If social cohesion is a necessary adjunct of national strength and national government, India has still far to go before she gazes on the promised land. One of the first duties of the leaders of all parties is to unteach partisanship; for the existing intolerance of each other's religious views and practices, shown by both Hindu and Musalman, the refusal of the higher castes to allow the children of low caste to share education and other facilities for social advancement, the harsher exhibitions of caste exclusiveness which frequently occur in all parts of India proper, the tendency among some of the upper and educated members of Indian society to regard the criminal law as primarily intended for the correction of only lower class misdoing—these and other unamiable symptoms of mediævalism are merely retarding the great cause which the Indian nationalist has at heart. They lead indirectly to crime; they militate directly against the growth of social order and a national conscience.

In the peculiar circumstances and conditions of India and its huge heterogeneous population, it is questionable whether the Government of the last few years has not extended its toleration of anti-social movements and disorder almost beyond the point of safety. In the remote tranquillity of a Himalayan hill-station, or in the security of Whitehall, with its barricades and Metropolitan constables, it is doubtless easy enough to speak of allowing a dangerous subversive movement to fail by reason of its own inanity.[1] Such a policy might conceivably be justified by results in a country with a homogeneous and educated population. But it cannot be otherwise than dangerous in India, where the vast mass of the people is uncivilized according to modern standards, and where large numbers of actual and potential criminals are ever ready to seize the first opportunity for resort to methods of violence and forms of crime inherited from past ages of rapine and violence. As must always happen when the central government vacillates or prefers rhetoric to action, the brunt of the struggle to maintain order and hold outrages in check falls upon an inadequate and scattered police force—a fact which has received ample corroboration in India since the year 1917. A little more determination

[1] See Lord Chelmsford's speech at the meeting of the Legislative Council in September, 1920.

to grapple sternly with lawlessness, a little less attention to immediate schemes for the political millennium in India, might have forestalled some of the atrocious tragedies of the last few years in that country. Yet the Indian policemen, who, because they were true to the salt of an alien Government, were savagely battered and burnt alive at Chauri-Chaura, Sholapur, and other places, will not have suffered their agony in vain, if their death serves to remind the Indian Government and their educated fellow-countrymen that the stern and swift suppression of disorder and crime is an essential concomitant of the progress and welfare of all States. Those Indians, who make the suppression of rioting an occasion for criticizing the executive authorities and for attacking the police, would do well to remember that the art of government was compendiously described in ancient India as being the Law of Punishment (*Dandaniti*), and that no less an authority than Manu declares:—

> 'Dread of the rod alone restrains the bad,
> Controls the good, and makes a nation happy . . .
> The king must therefore punish fearlessly;
> Else would the strong oppress the weak . . .
> The king is equally unjust who frees
> The guilty or condemns the innocent.'

FINIS

APPENDIX

(See page 92 *ante*)

"Shri Krishna."

New discovery!! Grand change in the physical phenomena.

The most systematic and scientific Society of Physical culture namely **Sri-Krishna Mission** will perform the following thunderous feats of strength and unseen wonderful powers in yoga in the Ripon theatre on Grant Road, Bombay, at 9-30 P. M. Standard time on Saturday the 9th of March 1912 **A.** D. and at 4 P. M. Standard time on Sunday the 10th of March 1912.

1. A distinct exibition of various muscles of the body.
2. Motor will be stopped by the stomach through yoga powers.
3. Various sorts of yoga postures will be shown.
4. A noose shall be given to the arms and chest by two motors and the actor shall resist the force by yoga powers.
5. Different sorts of club swinging exercises shall be exhibited.
6. Weight of 200 lbs. shall be thrown up on the chest from the height of 3 ft. and the actor will easily resist the deadly shock by yoga powers.
7. Two full loaded big carts will cross the fore-arms.
8. Weight of 240 lbs. shall be lifted by teeth through will power.

9. Two packs of playing cards shall be torn together.

10. The straight body will be thrown Horrizontally from the height of 5 ft. and the actor will bear the shock against the ground without any injury by yoga powers.

Besides these feats great weights shall be lifted by fingers and hands in different positions.

Rates of Tickets

		Rs.	A.	P.
1	Reserved Stalls 2 lines	3	0	0
2	„ Box „	2	0	0
3	Box	1	8	0
4	Stalls 2 lines	1	0	0
5	Stalls back lines	0	12	0
6	Gallary	0	8	0
7	Pit	0	4	0
	Ladies	0	4	0
	Prostitutes	1	0	0

Notice.—The smoking is strictly prohibited.

2. Doors will open at 8-30 P. M. Standard Time, and the feats will begin at 9-30 P. M. Standard Time.

3. The ticket that is once purchased shall not be retaken on any condition.

4. Children below the age of 10 shall have to pay half the charges.

5. The programme is liable to alteration.

6. The rates of the tickets will be increased according to the time.

7. Persons shall not be allowed according to our will.

8. Men behaving ungentlemanly shall be driven out without returning the money.

Tickets are available at the following places.

1. Ripon Theatre on Saturday at 8-30 P. M. St. T.
   „ Sunday at 2 P. M. St. T.
2. The lodging of S. M. every day till 6 P. M. S. T.

SHRI-KRISHNA MISSION,
Bhai Jiwanji's Lane,
Gokuldas Vithaldas Building, III Story, Thakurdwar.

Manager,
SHRI-KRISHNA MISSION.

N. B.—Persons wishing to see the hardness of bodily muscles personally on stage shall have to purchase special tickets worth Rs. 5.

Note.—The spelling, etc., is reproduced exactly as in the original handbill.

INDEX